The Complex PTSD Recovery Guide

Empowering Strategies to Manage Trauma, Build Trust and Support Emotional Well-being

Dane McRae

Dane McRae

Copyright ©2025

Dane McRae

Publisher: Dane McRae

TABLE OF CONTENTS

INTRODUCTION

In the quiet moments when you pause to look beyond the surface of daily life, you may face emotions and memories that seem inexplicable, yet they echo deep within. These feelings might be remnants of a journey marked by Complex Post-Traumatic Stress Disorder (Complex PTSD), a condition distinct from traditional PTSD. Imagine this as not just an extension of trauma but a shadow emerging from prolonged, repeated traumas often rooted in childhood. A child who has faced neglect or abuse might carry the weight of inadequacy and fear well into adulthood, struggling with an intricate web of emotional health challenges.

Understanding Complex PTSD begins with recognizing it as more than a set of symptoms—it's a legitimate outcome of trauma deserving comprehension and empathy. A crucial step in any recovery is validating these experiences, both for individuals navigating their own paths and for those walking alongside loved ones. The acknowledgment of early trauma's profound influence is not merely therapeutic; it's empowering, offering the first flickers of hope on the journey toward recovery.

This guide is crafted with compassion at its heart, serving as a beacon for those who feel lost in silence. You are not alone. These narrative shines light into the hidden corners, offering clarity where there was once confusion, by gently guiding you toward self-understanding and healing. Many endure the silent struggles of Complex PTSD, yet by coming together through shared insights, we illuminate the path forward, one marked by understanding and compassion.

Being aware of one's inner landscape is an invaluable asset in the healing process. Think of self-awareness as a lantern guiding you through the maze of your experiences. Simple self-assessment tools offer a starting point to untangle these complex layers. Ask yourself: What memories provoke intense emotions or reactions? By identifying these triggers, you build the foundation for meaningful change and healing.

This guide aims to serve as both an informative resource and a supportive companion, outlining strategies grounded in both psychological insight and practical application. We will delve into the intricacies of trauma and explore actionable steps to help you reclaim control over your story, fostering resilience and growth in the process. Each chapter is designed to open new doors to understanding, helping you navigate your personal journey with greater clarity and confidence.

Engagement with this material is not just recommended; it's essential. As you progress, allow yourself moments of introspection. Reflect on how the techniques discussed apply to your life. Consider what changes you can implement today to move delicately toward healing. Your personal experiences are at the forefront of this journey; they inform the way you interact with the strategies presented, enabling you to tailor them to suit your unique needs.

Healing, while possible, is undeniably a gradual process. Prepare yourself for a transformative journey of self-discovery and growth. Understand that progress is rarely linear—it often involves weaving through advancement and retreat. Yet, each small step you take brings you closer to becoming a more integrated and healthier self, providing glimpses of the vibrant person within that Complex PTSD has overshadowed.

Throughout this exploration, remember that patience and self-kindness are your greatest allies. Healing is a deeply personal experience, unfolding at its own pace. Just as no two stories are identical, neither are recovery processes. Embrace the nuances of your journey, finding strength in vulnerability and courage in every moment of reflection.

Friends and family members of those with Complex PTSD will find this guide equally beneficial. While they may stand on different ground—witnessing rather than directly experiencing the struggle—they play a crucial role in creating a supportive environment. Through understanding and empathy, they can help alleviate the isolation felt by their loved ones, advocating for a collective journey toward healing.

For mental health professionals and therapists, this book seeks to deepen your understanding of Complex PTSD, extending beyond the textbook definitions and diving into lived experiences. By exploring therapeutic strategies tailored specifically to this condition, you gain insights that will enhance your ability to guide clients sensitively and effectively toward recovery.

As you engage with the following pages, I invite you to embrace this opportunity for growth and reflection. Whether you're seeking to beĖer understand your journey, support someone dear, or refine your professional practice, this guide offers a framework for exploration and connection. Allow these insights to inspire and empower you on the path ahead.

With openness and dedication, the journey toward healing from Complex PTSD transforms from daunting to liberating. This book stands with you, each page a reminder that though the path may be challenging, you're never truly alone. Together, let's embark on this journey of healing and discovery, embracing each step as a testament to resilience and hope.

Understanding Complex PTSD

Understanding Complex PTSD involves navigating the intricate emotional landscape created by prolonged exposure to trauma. This condition, while sharing some characteristics with standard PTSD, delves deeper into changes in self-perception and personal relationships. As we explore the depths of Complex PTSD, it becomes evident that the ongoing nature of such trauma shapes both how individuals see themselves and interact with the world around them. The chapter invites readers into a journey to grasp the profound implications of prolonged traumatic experiences on the psyche and life dynamics.

Differences between PTSD and Complex PTSD

Understanding the differences between PTSD and Complex PTSD is crucial for those affected, their loved ones, and professionals. While both conditions are reactions to trauma, Complex PTSD involves more extensive identity changes due to prolonged exposure to traumatic situations. This distinction becomes evident when examining their diagnostic criteria, which reveal that Complex PTSD often results in pervasive impacts on a person's sense of self.

Unlike PTSD, which might result from a single traumatic event, Complex PTSD develops from sustained and repeated exposure to trauma, such as long-term abuse or captivity. These experiences alter not only how individuals perceive themselves but also their ability to relate to others and the world around them. The resulting identity disturbances may manifest as feelings of worthlessness, deep-seated shame, or ongoing guilt. Those suffering from Complex PTSD may struggle with an internal dialogue that constantly questions their intrinsic value or identity.

One striking feature of Complex PTSD is the pronounced cognitive and emotional challenges it presents, particularly self-regulation difficulties. Individuals might find themselves frequently overwhelmed by emotions, unable to predict or control their emotional responses. This can lead to intense episodes of anxiety, anger, or sadness that seem disconnected from present circumstances. The ability to maintain a consistent emotional state becomes a daily baÈle, often further complicating other aspects of life, like work or relationships. For example, a person might suddenly experience waves of panic or anger over seemingly minor triggers, leaving them and those around them baffled by the intensity of their reaction.

Where standard PTSD might cause some degree of emotional dysregulation, the scope and depth within Complex PTSD are typically much greater. The brain and body's response to chronic trauma leaves behind a complex tapestry of emotional vulnerabilities and challenges. This hyper-reactivity requires thoughtful strategies to manage effectively, often involving therapeutic interventions targeted at developing healthier coping mechanisms. Understanding these dynamics is essential because it underscores why certain therapeutic approaches might work well for PTSD but fall short in addressing the nuanced needs of Complex PTSD patients.

Relational dynamics are another area where Complex PTSD significantly diverges from standard PTSD. The impact of trauma on personal relationships can be profound, creating paÈerns of avoidance, distrust, or fears of abandonment. Those with Complex PTSD often develop distorted perceptions of interpersonal relations. For instance, they might struggle with dependency issues, feeling excessively reliant on others while simultaneously fearing intimacy or rejection. Their past experiences teach them to anticipate harm even in safe environments, making it difficult to form lasting bonds.

In contrast, PTSD may not necessarily influence relational dynamics to the same extent, focusing more on the memories of a specific event rather than a fundamental alteration in interpersonal trust. The continuous trauma inherent to Complex PTSD rewires individuals' expectations and interactions with others, painting a landscape where every relationship feels fraught with potential danger. To navigate these challenges, it's vital to foster supportive connections and engage in therapies that emphasize building healthy relational skills.

In essence, the ongoing relational tension in Complex PTSD necessitates a multi-faceted approach that includes not just understanding and empathy from loved ones but also structured therapeutic support aimed at healing old wounds and establishing new, positive interaction paĖerns. Therapeutic modalities such as group therapy can be incredibly beneficial here, providing a space for sharing experiences and learning from others who face similar challenges.

Symptom Manifestations

Understanding the symptoms specifically linked to Complex PTSD is crucial for distinguishing it from standard PTSD and recognizing its profound impact on individuals. One significant symptom is emotional dysregulation, which often manifests as intense emotional responses that seem disproportionate to the situation at hand. Individuals with Complex PTSD may struggle to manage their emotions effectively, leading to mood swings, persistent sadness, or explosive anger. This can create a challenging environment both for the person experiencing these emotions and for those around them.

In Complex PTSD, disturbances in self-identity are also common. People may experience confusion about who they are or what they believe in, which can be disorienting and distressing. This disruption in identity often stems from prolonged exposure to trauma, where one's sense of self-worth is continuously undermined. They might feel a pervasive sense of failure or view themselves through a lens shaped by the abuse or neglect they have endured. This disturbance can lead to feelings of shame, guilt, and diminished self-esteem, making everyday interactions burdensome and reinforcing isolation.

Dissociation is another coping mechanism frequently utilized by those with Complex PTSD. It serves as an escape when emotions become overwhelming or memories too painful to bear consciously. Dissociation can manifest as a sense of detachment from reality, where individuals feel disconnected from their thoughts, feelings, bodies, or surroundings. This mental distancing allows them to separate from the trauma temporarily but can become disruptive if it happens frequently or without control. Those experiencing dissociation might describe feeling as though they are observing their life from outside their body or existing in a dream-like state—a vague unreality encasing their everyday experiences.

Adding further complexity to Complex PTSD are chronic feelings of helplessness and disconnection. Unlike traditional PTSD, where fear arises from specific triggers, Complex PTSD involves a more pervasive sense of powerlessness. The recurring trauma rewires belief systems, instilling a deep-seated conviction that one cannot change their circumstances. This sentiment makes it notably difficult for individuals to envision or pursue a future free from suffering. Consequently, even small challenges or changes may appear insurmountable, trapping them in cycles of despair.

This ongoing sense of disconnection frequently affects relationships. People with Complex PTSD might find it hard to trust others due to past betrayals or abuse. They may keep their guard up, fearing vulnerability will only lead to more pain. Therefore, maintaining close connections becomes arduous, as the very relationships that could offer healing instead trigger anxiety and suspicion. Their world can grow smaller as they retreat inward, seemingly safer within walls built by fear and mistrust.

While discussing these complex symptoms, it's vital to acknowledge strategies for coping and resilience. Developing skills in grounding techniques can help manage emotional dysregulation. Simple exercises such as focusing on breathing, using sensory stimuli like touch or sound, or engaging in physical activities can provide immediate relief by redirecting focus away from distressing emotions. These practices anchor the individual in the present moment, counteracting the whirlwind of overpowering feelings.

Building resilience despite the weight of Complex PTSD involves cultivating a supportive network. Engaging with loved ones or support groups where individuals feel heard, understood, and validated can promote a sense of belonging and acceptance. For those struggling with self-identity disturbances, therapy offers a safe space to explore and reconstruct one's self-perception. Therapists trained in trauma-informed approaches can guide clients in identifying negative beliefs shaped by trauma and replacing them with healthier narratives.

When addressing dissociation, mindfulness techniques hold particular value. Practices centered on staying present, such as meditation or mindful walking, encourage grounding in reality. By gradually increasing awareness and acceptance of their surroundings and emotional states, individuals can reduce the frequency and intensity of dissociative episodes. Therapy may also assist in uncovering and understanding underlying triggers, allowing individuals to anticipate and navigate potential situations that might elicit a dissociative response.

Chronic feelings of helplessness require intentional efforts to shift mindset and foster empowerment. Goal-setting and celebrating small achievements can break down the illusion of insurmountability that complex trauma builds. As individuals recognize their capacity for influence and change, they pave pathways towards reclaiming autonomy.

Finally, highlighting the importance of professional help is essential. Therapeutic interventions can address the multifaceted symptoms of Complex PTSD comprehensively, providing tools and therapies tailored to each individual's needs. Eye Movement Desensitization and Reprocessing (EMDR), Cognitive Behavioral Therapy (CBT), or Dialectical Behavior Therapy (DBT) are among approaches known to effect positive change in many people dealing with Complex PTSD.

Coping Mechanisms

Understanding how to cope with Complex PTSD involves examining different strategies compared to those used for standard PTSD. This is because the nature of the trauma and its effects vary significantly, requiring an adapted approach. For someone dealing with Complex PTSD, healing begins with recognizing that their experience often stems from prolonged trauma, which by nature demands a more nuanced, sustained method of healing. In contrast, standard PTSD typically arises from single, identifiable events, allowing for more straightforward therapeutic interventions.

A key component in addressing Complex PTSD is understanding that accumulated trauma necessitates navigation beyond typical PTSD treatments. Traditional approaches might not be as effective due to the intricacies involved with ongoing trauma. For example, standard methods such as exposure therapy, which work well with event-based PTSD, might not sufficiently address the deep-rooted paĖerns developed over years of repeated trauma exposure. Instead, therapies like prolonged exposure or EMDR (Eye Movement Desensitization and Reprocessing), often require adaptation when applied to complex cases, where safety, stability, and creating a nurturing therapeutic relationship are prioritized before delving into trauma narratives.

Moreover, it is critical to engage in multifaceted strategies for healing. Integrating approaches such as trauma-focused cognitive behavioral therapy (CBT) with other modalities, such as dialectical behavior therapy (DBT), can significantly bolster emotional regulation skills. This combination aids individuals in managing the intense emotions associated with Complex PTSD, especially as they work through past experiences and current triggers.

Diverse support systems play a substantial role in tackling the multifaceted nature of Complex PTSD. It's essential to recognize that support extends beyond professional therapy; it involves creating a circle of care that includes family, friends, and support groups who understand and empathize with the survivor's journey. Having multiple sources of support helps provide varied perspectives and coping tools, promoting resilience and emotional balance.

Support from loved ones isn't just beneficial; it can be transformative. When family members and friends are educated about Complex PTSD, they are beĖer equipped to offer meaningful assistance. This can include providing stable environments, being patient with emotional fluctuations, and encouraging healthy habits. Encouraging openness and building trust within these relationships fosters a sense of security crucial for those with Complex PTSD. It is also important for caregivers to practice self-care and maintain their own boundaries to sustain supportive roles effectively.

Additionally, integrating mindfulness and holistic practices can complement traditional therapies. Techniques like yoga, meditation, and breathing exercises promote grounding and present-moment awareness, which are invaluable in managing intrusive thoughts and emotional distress. Such practices empower individuals to develop internal resources for coping, enhancing their ability to self-soothe during overwhelming situations.

Incorporating creative outlets also provides another layer of healing. Art therapy, music, writing, or any form of creative expression can facilitate processing complex emotions nonverbally. These outlets allow for exploration and expression of feelings that might be difficult to articulate, offering a cathartic release that traditional talk therapies may not achieve alone.

The path to recovery is neither linear nor predictable. Each individual's journey with Complex PTSD is unique, requiring patients and practitioners alike to remain adaptable and sensitive to evolving needs. Realistic expectations and small, incremental steps toward progress should be celebrated, reinforcing hope and motivation.

Stigma and Misunderstanding

Complex PTSD is a deeply misunderstood condition, primarily due to the societal stigmas and misconceptions that cloud its perception. Unlike traditional PTSD, which often stems from a single traumatic event, Complex PTSD arises from prolonged exposure to trauma, such as ongoing abuse or captivity. This extended trauma leads to more pervasive psychological impacts, yet it remains less understood by society at large. The stigma surrounding mental health issues in general, and Complex PTSD in particular, can discourage individuals from seeking help, further exacerbating their struggles.

Many people hold misconceptions about the nature of Complex PTSD. They may perceive those with the disorder as simply overreacting or failing to move past their experiences. Such aĖitudes are not only incorrect but also harmful. They create an environment where individuals feel isolated and unsupported, making it difficult for them to come forward and share their experiences or seek therapy. By perpetuating these myths, society denies recognition of the legitimate challenges faced by those suffering from Complex PTSD.

Education plays a crucial role in dismantling these unhelpful stereotypes. When the public becomes more informed about the realities of Complex PTSD, empathy and support naturally follow. Educating others about the disorder involves sharing factual information about its causes, symptoms, and effects. It means explaining how long-term trauma can affect someone's ability to trust, regulate their emotions, and form relationships. Understanding these elements helps foster compassion and reduces judgment or dismissal of those impacted by Complex PTSD.

Furthermore, education empowers friends and family members to beÈer support their loved ones. When they comprehend the intricacies of Complex PTSD, they can engage in more meaningful conversations, provide appropriate encouragement, and accompany their loved ones on their journey toward healing. Mental health professionals also benefit from increased awareness, allowing them to refine their approaches and develop more effective therapeutic strategies tailored to the needs of their clients with Complex PTSD.

One powerful method of educating others involves sharing personal stories and testimonials. Hearing directly from those who have lived through prolonged trauma offers invaluable insights into the daily realities faced by individuals with Complex PTSD. These narratives illuminate the diverse ways the disorder manifests, revealing not just the pain but also the resilience and strength of those affected. Personal accounts highlight that recovery is neither linear nor simple, but rather a complex path that requires patience, understanding, and support.

Moreover, stories and testimonials bring a human face to a condition that can otherwise seem abstract or distant. They provide a window into the world of sufferers, helping others relate more personally to their struggles. This connection can inspire greater societal change, shifting perceptions and encouraging more inclusive and supportive environments for those navigating their recovery journeys.

By focusing on these aspects, we can begin to challenge and change the harmful misconceptions about Complex PTSD. With greater understanding comes the potential to offer genuine support and help those affected feel validated in their experiences and hopeful about their futures. Society as a whole benefits when its members are more aware and empathetic, fostering a culture where mental health issues are openly discussed without fear of judgment.

The Impact of Prolonged Trauma Exposure

Understanding the effects of prolonged trauma on psychological and emotional landscapes is essential in grasping the dynamics of Complex PTSD. Chronic trauma, which involves repeated and ongoing exposure to traumatic events, goes beyond the immediate mental and emotional distress, leaving a more profound imprint on brain function and structure. This physical validation of mental struggles highlights why individuals with Complex PTSD may experience symptoms differing from those exposed to a single traumatic event.Scientific studies suggest that chronic trauma impacts areas of the brain involved in stress response, emotion regulation, and memory processing. For instance, the amygdala, responsible for detecting threats, can become overactive, leading to heightened anxiety and fear responses. Meanwhile, the hippocampus, crucial for forming new memories, might shrink in volume, affecting the ability to distinguish past experiences from present realities. These changes underscore how deeply ingrained trauma becomes over time, influencing behaviors and perceptions long after the removal from the traumatic environment.

Trust deficits often emerge as another consequence of prolonged trauma exposure. People who have endured continuous trauma frequently find it challenging to trust others, originating from repeated betrayals or inconsistent support during traumatic events. This lack of trust can manifest in personal relationships, making it difficult for sufferers to form healthy connections. Such relational paÉerns are not only based on the anticipation of harm but also on learned self-protective mechanisms developed to survive previous adversities.

Unhealthy relational paÉerns can further complicate recovery by perpetuating cycles of mistrust and isolation. Individuals with Complex PTSD might unintentionally sabotage close relationships, fearing vulnerability will lead to more hurt. As a result, they may gravitate towards unhealthy aÉachments or remain in toxic dynamics, reinforcing their expectations of betrayal and disappointment. Recognizing and breaking these paÉerns requires both self-awareness and supportive interventions tailored to building safety and trust.

Trauma's impact on self-esteem and self-perception forms another layer of complexity for those experiencing Complex PTSD. The negative messages internalized during traumatic periods can warp a person's view of themselves, leading to destructive self-beliefs. For example, someone who has been repeatedly told they are inadequate or unworthy during abuse might start to genuinely believe this narrative, affecting their self-worth and confidence.

These internalized negative beliefs can be so pervasive that they influence every aspect of an individual's life, from career choices to social interactions. Breaking free from this distorted self-image often involves challenging deeply embedded thoughts and replacing them with healthier affirmations. This process can be arduous and require considerable emotional lifting, underscoring the need for compassionate guidance from therapists or support groups specializing in trauma recovery.

While acknowledging these challenges, it's critical to recognize the potential for healing and transformation. Adaptive vs. maladaptive coping mechanisms play a significant role in shaping one's journey toward recovery. While maladaptive strategies may initially provide temporary relief from distress—such as avoidance or substance abuse—they ultimately hinder healing by maintaining individuals in a state of unresolved trauma. Conversely, adaptive coping techniques foster resilience and enable sustainable recovery. This might include activities like mindfulness meditation, which helps in grounding and reconnecting with the present moment, or expressive therapies such as art or music therapy, allowing for safe emotional expression. SeÈing small, achievable goals can also empower individuals by providing clear markers of progress and rebuilding a sense of control over one's life.

For friends and family members aÈempting to support loved ones with Complex PTSD, fostering empathy and understanding can significantly aid their recovery. It's vital to approach conversations with patience and an open mind, avoiding judgments or pressuring the individual to 'move on.' Instead, actively listening and providing consistent reassurance can help alleviate feelings of isolation and distrust.

Family members and friends should educate themselves about Complex PTSD to beÈer understand its intricacies and challenges. By doing so, they can offer informed support, helping create a nurturing environment conducive to healing. Empathy, patience, and education work hand-in-hand to dismantle the walls of distrust and fear, paving the way for genuine connection and understanding.

Mental health professionals aiming to guide clients through recovery must consider the unique nuances of Complex PTSD. Therapy models like trauma-focused cognitive-behavioral therapy (TF-CBT) or eye movement desensitization and reprocessing (EMDR) can be particularly effective. These therapies provide structured approaches to address both the emotional and cognitive aspects of trauma, enabling clients to process distressing memories in a safe and controlled manner.

Furthermore, integrating a holistic perspective into treatment plans, considering factors such as nutrition, exercise, and social engagement, can enhance overall well-being and support the healing process. Encouraging clients to build strong, positive networks with peers who understand similar struggles can ease feelings of alienation and boost morale.

Recognizing the Symptoms

Recognizing symptoms is the gateway to understanding the intricate journey of Complex PTSD. It involves a keen awareness and aĖention to how our mind and body respond to past trauma. This chapter invites you into a reflective space, exploring the myriad ways one can identify these often elusive signs within oneself. Through self-assessment techniques that serve as filters through which emotions and experiences are sifted, individuals will find a path to greater clarity and insight.

Self-Assessment Techniques

Recognizing and accurately identifying symptoms is a crucial first step in the journey towards recovery from Complex PTSD. One effective method to begin this exploration involves the use of symptom checklists. These tools serve as a clear guide for individuals seeking to understand their emotional and psychological response paĖerns. By systematically reviewing a list of potential symptoms, individuals can pinpoint specific behaviors, thoughts, or feelings that might otherwise go unnoticed. This process not only aids in self-awareness but also facilitates conversations with mental health professionals who can offer guidance tailored to one's experiences.

Implementing a symptom checklist allows individuals to engage actively in their own Mental Health management. It serves as a personal inventory that highlights areas requiring aĖention and care. It opens up pathways to deeper understanding by encouraging reflection on how these symptoms manifest in daily life. For instance, a checklist item might include "frequent flashbacks," which can prompt an individual to recall specific instances where they have experienced such episodes, providing critical insights into triggers and paĖerns.

Journaling emerges as another powerful tool for those navigating the intricate web of trauma responses. The practice of writing down thoughts and feelings regularly allows individuals to track recurring themes related to their emotional state. Over time, journaling can reveal paĖerns, such as persistent feelings of anxiety when encountering certain social situations, enabling individuals to connect these occurrences to their trauma history. In addition to recognizing paĖerns, journaling fosters emotional clarity and understanding. It transforms abstract emotions into tangible words, helping individuals articulate what might be difficult to express verbally.

Through journaling, people can also record their progress, offering a historical perspective on their evolving mental health. This reflective process does more than just identify symptoms; it encourages growth and healing by documenting personal stories of resilience and change. Creating a dedicated space for these reflections not only supports individuals in navigating their complex emotional landscapes but also serves as a valuable resource for therapists who may use these insights to tailor therapeutic interventions.

In addition to internal strategies like checklists and journaling, seeking feedback from trusted individuals adds another layer of perspective to recognizing symptoms. Family members, friends, or supportive colleagues often notice behavior changes that an individual might overlook. These external observations can validate or challenge one's self-assessment, offering a broader view of how symptoms affect interactions and relationships.

Inviting feedback requires a willingness to listen openly and aĖentively. It also calls for creating a safe environment where loved ones feel comfortable sharing their honest observations. This mutual exchange not only strengthens bonds but also enhances the support network essential for recovery. Encouraging loved ones to share their insights can lead to revelations about overlooked behavioral paÈerns, promoting greater self-awareness and adjustment.

In today's digital age, technology offers additional resources to aid in symptom recognition. Numerous apps and online platforms are designed to facilitate mood and emotion tracking, providing real-time data and analysis. These tools provide visual representations of mood fluctuations over days, weeks, or even months, offering users a detailed picture of their emotional well-being.

By inputting daily mood reports, individuals gain access to analytics that highlight potential triggers or stressors affecting their mental health. Many apps also include features for seÈing reminders for mindfulness practices or recording brief diary entries, blending technology seamlessly with traditional methods like journaling. These platforms can extend the reach of self-monitoring, offering anonymous communities where users share experiences and coping strategies, fostering a sense of connection and shared understanding among individuals with similar struggles.

While each method — whether checklists, journaling, feedback, or digital monitoring — stands strong individually, their combined use amplifies the potential for thorough symptom recognition. They each contribute uniquely to an integrated approach that caters to varied needs and preferences. Incorporating multiple techniques provides a comprehensive toolkit for identifying symptoms, encouraging individuals to find what resonates most with them personally.

As individuals explore these methods, it's important to remain patient and kind with oneself. Recognition is just the beginning of the healing journey, and embracing each step with compassion can create space for growth and acceptance. Building this foundation is critical not only for individuals but also for mental health professionals and support networks striving to understand the complexities of Complex PTSD.

Understanding Symptom Checklists

In the journey to understand Complex PTSD, recognizing symptoms is crucial. By identifying specific signs through established criteria, individuals can beÉer navigate their healing process. One effective tool in this endeavor is the use of checklists. These lists serve as a compass, helping individuals pinpoint consistent emotional or mental health issues that might otherwise go unnoticed. They offer a structured way to capture and evaluate different paÉerns of behavior and emotions that recur over time.

Checklists are not just for those experiencing symptoms but also provide insight for friends, family, and mental health professionals. For individuals diagnosed with Complex PTSD, these lists can be empowering. Self-awareness fosters empowerment, and recognizing symptoms is the first step toward reclaiming one's life. By regularly consulting checklists, individuals become more attuned to their inner world, gaining clarity about what they experience on a daily basis.

Cross-referencing personal experiences with standardized lists can make symptom recognition an engaging process rather than an overwhelming one. This act allows individuals to see how their unique experiences align with broader paÉerns. It's like piecing together a puzzle where each piece represents a facet of their journey. Moreover, this comparison highlights areas that require aÉention, prompting them to seek the necessary support.

For individuals, having a checklist offers a sense of validation. Rather than wondering if certain feelings or reactions are normal, they find confirmation and understanding. It's comforting to know that there are established criteria that explain why they feel a certain way, and that those criteria are shared by others. Each item checked off is a step toward understanding and healing.

The empowerment through symptom identification paves the way for initial recovery steps. When individuals identify their symptoms, they can take deliberate actions toward managing them. They learn which aspects of their life need adjustment, whether it be lifestyle changes, coping strategies, or seeking professional help. This newfound insight serves as a catalyst for change. As they recognize symptoms, they build a roadmap to recovery, highlighting what needs attention and how to address it effectively.

Highlighting the use of checklists becomes particularly significant when initiating conversations with professionals. Entering therapy with a clear list of observed symptoms allows for more productive sessions. It equips both the individual and the therapist with a concrete starting point. Discussions become focused and targeted, reducing the ambiguity that often clouds therapeutic encounters.

Professionals can gain valuable insights from these checklists, enabling them to tailor interventions to the individual's specific needs. The practical benefit is clear: understanding someone's struggle in terms of established criteria can streamline therapeutic approaches, ensuring that treatment is as effective as possible. Checklists thus act as bridges between personal experience and professional guidance.

Moreover, these lists can foster open communication within support networks. Friends and family can beÉer understand the individual's condition when presented with concise information. Through shared checklists, loved ones can appreciate the seriousness of the symptoms without feeling overwhelmed by complex explanations. This understanding promotes empathy and patience, enhancing relationships and providing a supportive environment for the individual pursuing recovery.

A checklist isn't only a personal tool; it's a communal one that encourages dialogue. It invites questions, discussions, and shared learning experiences among all involved parties. Whether it's a friend learning about triggers or a therapist narrowing down therapeutic techniques, checklists facilitate informed conversations that move everyone forward.

Ultimately, embracing checklists in the context of Complex PTSD goes beyond mere identification—it fosters a proactive approach to healing. Recognizing symptoms is essential, but acting upon them is transformative. These lists serve as practical guides in the pursuit of well-being, helping individuals understand their condition, engage meaningfully with professionals, and maintain supportive relationships. By illuminating potential symptoms through established criteria, checklists lead individuals on a path to recovery, turning confusion into clarity and uncertainty into empowerment.

Importance of Early Recognition

Recognizing symptoms early in the context of Complex PTSD is not just about addressing an illness; it's a crucial step towards reclaiming control over one's life. Early detection can significantly impact recovery, providing individuals with the tools they need to engage proactively with their healing journey. By being vigilant and aÉentive to the onset of symptoms, one can prevent the further escalation of distressing manifestations that might otherwise spiral out of control.

When symptoms are recognized promptly, coping strategies can be implemented effectively, acting as a buffer to mitigate more severe problems down the line. This preemptive approach empowers individuals to manage their emotional health actively, rather than reacting passively to issues only once they've intensified. Imagine being able to anticipate potential emotional downturns or periods of heightened anxiety before they fully take root. This foresight can be transformational, offering individuals a means to chart a course for their mental well-being before the storm hits.

Furthermore, recognizing symptoms at an early stage facilitates timely intervention and engagement with mental health services. Many people living with Complex PTSD often hesitate to seek help, thinking that their symptoms aren't 'severe enough' to warrant professional aĖention. However, by identifying these symptoms early, individuals provide themselves the opportunity to explore therapeutic options when they might be most effective. This not only enhances the potential outcomes of treatment but also allows for a more nuanced understanding of the condition itself. For example, therapy sessions can focus on building specific skills and strategies tailored to the individual's unique needs, leading to a more personalized path to recovery.

In addition to engaging with mental health professionals, early recognition plays a pivotal role in building self-awareness. Understanding one's own trauma responses can lead to a deeper comprehension of personal triggers and emotional paĖerns. This self-awareness is vital in fostering resilience. When individuals recognize how their past experiences shape their current behavior, they can begin to reframe their narratives and make conscious choices that align with their desired emotional state. Consider someone who notices recurring feelings of fear or anger without apparent cause. By tracing these emotions back to underlying trauma, they can address the root rather than merely treating the symptom.

Such awareness also aids in navigating relationship dynamics, which can often become strained due to misunderstandings or miscommunications stemming from unaddressed trauma responses. By improving interactions with loved ones through the lens of early symptom recognition, individuals can foster healthier, more supportive relationships. For instance, someone who understands their tendency to withdraw during stress due to past experiences can communicate this to their partner, transforming potential conflict into an opportunity for connection and mutual support.

Moreover, early symptom recognition helps demystify the experience of Complex PTSD for both the affected individual and those supporting them. It encourages open dialogues about difficult emotions and behaviors, removing the stigma that so often surrounds mental health issues. Friends and family members, equipped with knowledge about potential symptoms and their meanings, can provide beĖer support. They become allies in the recovery process rather than mere spectators, aiding their loved ones through the complexities of healing.

For mental health professionals, understanding the importance of early symptom recognition can enhance therapeutic practices. Therapists can guide clients in developing insights into their condition from the outset, emphasizing proactive engagement over reactive crisis management. This shift not only benefits individual clients but also contributes to broader trends in mental health care, where prevention and early intervention are increasingly valued alongside traditional therapeutic methods.

Journaling for Self-Discovery

Reflective writing can serve as a transformative tool for individuals navigating the complexities of Complex PTSD. By committing to document and assess mental health over time, one can develop a deeper understanding of their own emotional landscape. Journaling offers a private and personal space where thoughts and feelings can be expressed freely, without judgment or external pressure. This practice encourages self-reflection, allowing individuals to recognize patterns in their emotional responses and understand how they change over time.

The act of journaling can help identify recurring themes related to trauma. Over time, looking back at past entries may reveal consistent emotional triggers or responses that were not immediately apparent. These patterns can provide valuable insight into the underlying issues that perpetuate distressing symptoms. For instance, frequent mentions of anxiety in social situations might highlight an unresolved fear stemming from past experiences. Recognizing these patterns empowers individuals to address them proactively, equipping them with the knowledge needed to break free from cycles of negative emotions and work towards healing.

In addition to identifying paĖerns, reflective writing promotes emotional clarity and understanding. The process of penning down thoughts forces an individual to organize and articulate their emotions, providing a clearer picture of what they are experiencing. This clarity is crucial in differentiating between PTSD-related emotions and other stressors, enabling beĖer management of one's mental health. Writing about an overwhelming feeling of sadness, for example, might uncover connections between current emotions and past traumatic events, facilitating a deeper understanding of oneself.

Creating a personal historical record of mental health progression through journaling is another significant benefit. As individuals continue their journey, being able to review past entries provides perspective on growth and change. It serves as a tangible reminder of personal resilience and progress, even when days seem dark. This historical record can be particularly motivating; seeing how far one has come instills hope and reinforces commitment to recovery. Moreover, having this documented history can be invaluable during therapy sessions, offering mental health professionals a more comprehensive view of the individual's journey and aiding in tailored treatment approaches.

Journaling also aids in the processing of complex emotions. Through writing, individuals can explore feelings they may find difficult to express verbally. This exploration allows for a safe release of pent-up emotions, reducing internal stress and promoting mental well-being. Over time, consistent journaling may foster a sense of emotional regulation, making it easier to handle intense emotional experiences associated with PTSD.

Additionally, keeping a journal offers the opportunity for creative expression. Engaging in storytelling, poetry, or even sketching within journal pages can further enhance the therapeutic benefits of writing. Creative expression provides a different lens through which individuals can view their experiences, often leading to new insights and perspectives that might not surface through traditional methods of reflection. This creative outlet can become a source of comfort and pleasure, balancing the introspective aspects of journaling with moments of artistic freedom.

For friends and family members supporting loved ones with Complex PTSD, encouraging the practice of reflective writing can be a gentle way to aid in their journey. Providing a supportive environment where individuals feel comfortable sharing their wriÉen thoughts (if they wish) can strengthen relationships and build trust. It's important for supporters to respect privacy, recognizing that journaling is ultimately a personal endeavor meant for self-discovery and healing.

Mental health professionals can also integrate reflective writing into therapeutic strategies. Encouraging clients to maintain a journal provides an additional layer of support outside of sessions, fostering continuity in self-reflection and insight-building. Reviewing journal entries together can facilitate discussions around progress, challenges, and goals, enhancing overall treatment efficacy.

Seeking Feedback from Trusted Individuals

Understanding and recognizing the symptoms of Complex PTSD is crucial in navigating the path to healing. One vital aspect of this process is the consideration of external perspectives on one's self-perception. Often, individuals may embark on a journey of self-assessment, seeking to understand their feelings and behaviors. While this internal reflection is essential, it can be profoundly beneficial to validate these insights through the observations and input from friends or family.

Imagine you are looking at yourself in a mirror. Your reflection provides a certain view, but there might be facets of your appearance that are hidden from your sight. Similarly, when assessing your own mental health symptoms, there may be dimensions that are not immediately visible to you but can be recognized by those around you. Friends and family members who spend time with you observe paEerns in your behavior that you might overlook or dismiss as insignificant. Their observations can serve as a valuable guidepost, confirming or challenging your self-assessments and helping you see a more complete picture of your emotional landscape.

Recognizing overlooked paEerns pointed out by others can be an enlightening experience. For instance, a friend might notice that you tend to withdraw from social activities without apparent reason, which could be a symptom you haven't fully acknowledged. Such feedback can bring awareness to recurring patterns or triggers you hadn't identified on your own. This external input can act as a flashlight, illuminating areas of your mental well-being that require aEention, enabling you to take targeted actions towards management and healing.

Fostering a supportive network is another integral component of symptom recognition. Building such a network involves surrounding yourself with people who are not only willing to offer their perspectives but do so in a manner that feels safe and non-judgmental. This network could include intimate friends, family members, or even support groups where shared experiences create a collective understanding. In these spaces, vulnerability is nurtured, allowing for open discussions about mental health struggles. The input from this network can provide additional clarity and validation, reinforcing the idea that you are not alone in your journey. This shared space cultivates strength, as knowing others recognize and validate your experiences can be profoundly comforting and motivating.

Encouraging openness to feedback is pivotal for relational support and growth. It requires cultivating an aEitude of receptiveness and curiosity rather than defensiveness. Receiving feedback, especially regarding sensitive topics like mental health, can feel daunting. However, approaching feedback with an open heart and mind can transform potential discomfort into opportunities for connection and insight. Understanding that genuine feedback often stems from care and concern allows you to embrace it as a tool for growth. It's about creating a dialogue, where feedback becomes a two-way street: both sharing and listening form the crux of meaningful relationships. This interaction can lead to deeper understanding, compassion, and empathy between you and your supporters, contributing positively to your healing process.

Incorporating external perspectives into your self-assessment isn't about relinquishing control over your personal narrative. Instead, it is an acknowledgment that our experiences and self-perceptions can be wonderfully complemented by the views of those who care for us. It enriches the tapestry of our self-awareness, adding depth and dimension. Engaging with these perspectives doesn't negate your autonomy; rather, it empowers you with comprehensive insights, fostering a balanced outlook on your journey with Complex PTSD.

Moreover, involving external perspectives in symptom recognition can demystify and destigmatize conversations about mental health within your circle. As loved ones contribute their observations, they become more attuned to the nuances of Complex PTSD, promoting a shared language around mental health that is informed and compassionate. This cultural shift within your immediate environment can have lasting impacts, encouraging ongoing support and understanding.

It is also essential to establish boundaries within these interactions, ensuring that feedback received is respectful and constructive. Clear communication about what type of feedback is helpful and appropriate sets the stage for positive exchanges. Mutual respect and understanding enhance these dialogues, making them beneficial rather than overwhelming.

Navigating Emotional Triggers

Navigating emotional triggers involves understanding one's own emotional landscape and developing strategies to manage these responses in a healthier way. Emotional triggers are deeply personal, often stemming from past experiences that can evoke intense reactions. Recognizing these triggers is the first step towards gaining control over them. The journey of managing emotions is not about eliminating feelings but rather learning how to respond to them constructively. It requires patience and self-awareness as well as the willingness to explore various coping mechanisms. This chapter guides readers through the complexities of emotional regulation by providing empathetic insights into the nature of triggers and how they influence behavior.

Building Coping Skills

Understanding various types of coping strategies is a foundational step in managing emotional triggers effectively. Coping strategies can broadly be classified into adaptive and maladaptive methods. Adaptive strategies are those that promote well-being, allowing individuals to process emotions constructively, ultimately leading to healthier psychological outcomes. Examples include mindfulness practices, exercise, social support, and creative outlets, all of which provide constructive channels for emotional energy.

On the other hand, maladaptive strategies may provide immediate relief but often worsen emotional distress over time. These might include avoidance behaviors, substance abuse, or excessive isolation, which can hinder long-term recovery and emotional growth. Recognizing the differences between these two types of strategies is crucial as it helps individuals choose pathways that lead to sustainable emotional regulation, rather than temporary fixes that might lead to further issues.

It's important to recognize that the effectiveness of coping mechanisms can vary greatly based on individual experiences and specific emotional triggers. What works well for one person might not necessarily be effective for another. This personalization is critical because everyone's journey with Complex PTSD is unique. Factors such as personal history, current life circumstances, and even personality traits play a significant role in determining which coping strategies will be most beneficial.

For example, someone who finds solace in solitary activities may benefit from journaling or art therapy, while another person might thrive in environments that offer communal support, such as group therapy or peer support groups. Exploring different coping strategies allows individuals to tailor their approach to fit their specific needs, enhancing the likelihood of finding methods that truly resonate and provide relief.

Developing self-awareness is another vital step towards managing emotional triggers more effectively. Awareness of one's current coping strategies can serve as a catalyst for change, guiding individuals toward healthier alternatives. To foster this awareness, individuals can begin by observing their natural responses to stressors and considering whether these responses align with their long-term goals of emotional recovery.

This reflection might reveal paÈerns of behavior that have gone unnoticed, such as a tendency to withdraw when feeling overwhelmed or to resort to negative self-talk. By identifying these paÈerns, individuals can work towards replacing less helpful strategies with more adaptive practices. For many, small incremental changes, such as incorporating short breathing exercises during moments of stress, can pave the way for more significant behavioral shifts.

Guidelines can be helpful in progressing through this self-awareness journey. Creating a simple chart noting common situations, feelings, reactions, and the outcomes they lead to can serve as a powerful tool. This practice encourages introspection and provides tangible evidence of progress, helping individuals acknowledge improvements and areas needing further aÉention.

Finally, learning to choose adaptive methods is essential for recovery. The path to healing involves embracing techniques that not only alleviate immediate discomfort but also foster resilience and emotional stability over time. Practicing strategies such as controlled breathing, progressive muscle relaxation, or developing a gratitude routine can equip individuals with tools needed to navigate emotional challenges more effectively.

Furthermore, understanding that choosing adaptive methods requires patience and perseverance is key. It's natural for individuals to experience setbacks or relapses into old habits, especially when encountering particularly challenging triggers. However, each effort to employ healthier coping strategies builds strength and confidence, promoting ongoing recovery.

Emotional Self-Tracking

Understanding and managing emotional triggers is an essential part of the healing journey for those with Complex PTSD. Developing tools to monitor emotional states gives individuals the power to transform their emotional responses. This transformation begins with self-awareness, which can be cultivated through methods such as journaling or utilizing digital applications designed to track emotions.

Keeping a journal serves as a reflective practice that allows individuals to document their day-to-day experiences. It provides a safe space to record thoughts and feelings as they occur, helping to pinpoint specific events or interactions that trigger emotional responses. For some, this might mean writing in a traditional notebook, while others may find comfort in the privacy offered by digital apps that encourage real-time entries. These digital tools often provide prompts and reminders, making it easier to stay consistent with the practice. By documenting these moments regularly, paEerns begin to emerge, offering valuable insights into one's emotional landscape.

Identifying paEerns in emotional reactions plays a crucial role in gaining an understanding of one's emotional journey. Over time, recurring themes or common scenarios that lead to distress can become apparent. For instance, recognizing that interactions with certain people consistently provoke anxiety could reveal underlying issues related to past trauma. Similarly, noticing an increase in stress levels during specific times of day might point to physiological or environmental factors at play. Identifying these paEerns not only fosters insight but also encourages a more profound comprehension of how past experiences shape current emotional responses.

This deeper understanding lays the groundwork for creating tailored strategies to manage emotional triggers effectively. Once paEerns are identified, individuals can work on developing personalized coping mechanisms that align with their unique experiences and needs. For example, someone who discovers that crowded places trigger their symptoms may choose to practice deep breathing exercises before entering such environments. Others might develop affirmations or mental checklists to steer their emotions in healthier directions when faced with specific situations. Tailoring strategies to individual needs ensures they are more likely to succeed, enhancing the therapeutic process and promoting emotional resilience.

Proactive coping becomes increasingly feasible by recognizing triggers and responses early in the emotional cycle. Awareness is a powerful tool—it allows individuals to anticipate and prepare for potential triggers rather than simply reacting to them after the fact. This proactive approach can significantly reduce the intensity of emotional responses. Consider someone who identifies anger as a recurring response to feeling marginalized in group discussions. Recognizing this paÉern equips them to employ strategies—such as mindful breathing, positive reframing, or practicing assertive communication—before the anger escalates. These steps mitigate the risk of overwhelming emotions taking control, empowering individuals to navigate through challenging situations with greater ease and confidence.

Guidelines play a pivotal role in transforming these concepts into actionable steps. Encouraging individuals to maintain consistency in their journaling or app usage is crucial. Set aside a specific time each day dedicated to reflecting on the day's experiences and emotional reactions. Whether it's first thing in the morning or just before bed, establishing a routine can solidify this habit, providing a reliable framework for tracking emotions.

Additionally, when identifying patterns, choosing a method of review that suits personal preferences is important. This could involve weekly reflections summarizing emotional highs and lows or monthly reviews identifying broader trends. Both approaches offer structured insight into how different variables influence emotional health.

When tailoring strategies, consultation with mental health professionals is invaluable. Therapists and counselors can offer guidance and validation, ensuring that chosen strategies are both effective and healthy. They can also introduce new techniques or suggest modifications to existing ones based on professional expertise and knowledge of Complex PTSD.

Finally, seÉing specific goals around proactive coping enhances motivation and accountability. These goals can range from reducing the duration of emotional episodes to implementing a new coping strategy each week. Keeping a record of achievements and progress reinforces the sense of empowerment, building a foundation of success that supports ongoing recovery efforts.

Grounding Techniques

Grounding exercises are simple yet powerful techniques designed to anchor individuals back into the present moment, particularly when intense emotions threaten to overwhelm. These exercises serve as immediate interventions, providing a temporary sanctuary from the swirling chaos of an emotional storm. For those grappling with Complex PTSD, grounding can be a lifeline—a tool to stabilize and regain control when the world seems to spin too fast.

Immediate intervention through grounding is crucial because it interrupts the cycle of overwhelming emotions before they spiral out of control. Imagine finding yourself in a situation where stress levels skyrocket; it could be triggered by an unexpected memory or a sensory cue that sends your mind racing. Employing a grounding exercise at this moment acts like hiÉing a mental pause button, offering a brief respite to collect thoughts and emotions. One such technique involves focusing on your senses to draw aÉention away from distressing thoughts. You may start by identifying and naming five things you can see around you. This activity shifts your concentration from internal turmoil to the external environment, reorienting your perceptions.

Reconnecting with the present moment not only prevents dissociative responses but also reinforces the notion that you are safe and in control. Dissociation often occurs as a defense mechanism, a way for the mind to escape when reality becomes too harsh. However, remaining grounded helps maintain the connection between mind and body, reducing the feeling of detachment. Simple exercises, such as taking deep breaths, placing your hand over your heart, and reminding yourself where you are, can be incredibly effective. By engaging in these actions, you reaffirm your presence in the current moment, breaking the cycle of disconnection before it fully takes hold.

A vital aspect of grounding is its adaptability and ease of practice, which can occur anywhere, anytime. Whether you are sitting at your desk, walking through a crowded space, or lying in bed, grounding exercises can be adjusted to suit the situation. This versatility enhances familiarity and effectiveness over time. Practicing regularly ensures that when the need arises, you are well-equipped to implement the technique effortlessly. Engaging in consistent practice is akin to building muscle memory, a process that requires repetition until an action becomes instinctive. Over time, what begins as a conscious effort will transform into an automatic response—an invaluable skill in moments of emotional turbulence.

Grounding exercises are not merely quick fixes; they are essential tools in maintaining emotional regulation. By integrating these practices into daily life, individuals create a foundation of stability upon which they can rely during periods of instability. Establishing a routine that includes grounding might involve seEing aside a few minutes each day dedicated solely to mindful awareness, allowing room for reflection and self-care. This structured approach equips individuals with the ability to navigate tumultuous emotions while fostering resilience and a sense of empowerment.

For example, the "5-4-3-2-1" technique is a practical grounding exercise that employs all five senses to help reconnect with the here and now. The exercise invites you to identify five items you can see, four you can touch, three you can hear, two you can smell, and one you can taste. Each step requires focused aEention, gradually easing the mind back into the present. By shifting awareness to tangible surroundings, it diverts focus from emotional distress, promoting calmness and clarity.

Another grounding method is the use of guided imagery, which involves envisioning a peaceful, safe place in rich detail. This visualization allows you to mentally 'visit' an environment where you feel secure and relaxed. Immersing oneself in this picturesque scene encourages relaxation and provides an escape from pressing anxieties. With regular practice, recalling this imagery can become a soothing retreat during moments of heightened emotion, acting as a mental oasis amidst life's unpredictability.

To enhance grounding efficacy, incorporating tactile elements can add another layer of support. Holding a textured object or squeezing a stress ball engages the sense of touch, further solidifying the connection to the present. Alternatively, immersing hands in cold water or softly tapping fingers against one another introduces a novel sensation that anchors awareness to the physical body rather than floating thoughts.

Developing a repertoire of grounding techniques is like assembling a personalized toolkit, adaptable for diverse situations and emotions. As each individual responds differently, experimentation may be necessary to discover what resonates most. Keeping a journal of experiences with various exercises can offer valuable insights into their impact, facilitating adjustments and refinements.

Creating a Trigger Management Plan

Creating a structured plan for managing emotional triggers is vital in navigating Complex PTSD. The first step involves compiling a comprehensive list of personal triggers and understanding their impacts. Each individual has unique stimuli that can provoke distressing emotional responses, often rooted in past traumatic experiences. Identifying these triggers requires careful reflection and self-awareness. It's beneficial to note not just the situations or environments that act as triggers, but also the internal cues such as specific thoughts, feelings, or body sensations. For individuals with Complex PTSD, recognizing how these elements interconnect can illuminate paÉerns and provide insight into why certain triggers have more significant impacts than others.

Once the list of triggers is established, it's crucial to delve into how each trigger specifically affects emotional and physical states. This exploration involves observing changes in mood, behavior, and thought processes when a trigger is encountered. Understanding these reactions can shed light on the underlying fears and vulnerabilities that fuel them. It is important to approach this process with compassion and patience, acknowledging that each reaction is valid and often a protective response to past trauma. By mapping out the consequences of each trigger, individuals can begin to anticipate their responses beÉer and devise strategies to mitigate these effects.

After identifying personal triggers and their impacts, establishing actionable steps for when a trigger arises becomes essential. Having pre-determined actions can significantly enhance control during triggering situations. Actionable steps might include practicing deep breathing exercises, engaging in grounding techniques, or removing oneself from a stressful environment temporarily. These actions serve as immediate interventions, preventing the escalation of emotional responses. Additionally, incorporating mindfulness practices can help maintain present awareness, reducing the grip of overwhelming emotions. Tailoring these steps to suit one's unique needs and comfort levels ensures they are practical and effective when needed most.

Incorporating support systems and resources within the plan is another critical component. Support systems may include trusted friends, family members, or mental health professionals who can provide reassurance and guidance. Connecting with others who understand or have similar experiences can offer validation and a sense of solidarity. Resources such as therapy sessions, support groups, or online communities also play a crucial role in broadening one's coping toolkit. These resources provide opportunities to learn new strategies, share insights, and receive encouragement during challenging times. Integrating these supports into the plan offers multiple avenues for assistance, ensuring that help is accessible whenever necessary.

Additionally, regularly reviewing and updating the plan for relevance and effectiveness is paramount. Emotional landscapes are not static; they evolve as healing progresses and life circumstances change. What worked at one time may require adjustments to remain effective. Regularly revisiting the plan ensures it aligns with current needs and continues to meet intended goals. During check-ins, it's valuable to reflect on recent experiences, assess the efficacy of previously established steps, and incorporate any newly acquired coping skills. Flexibility in modifying the plan allows for adaptation to both expected and unforeseen challenges, reinforcing resilience over time.

Moreover, being proactive about evaluating the plan creates a sense of empowerment. It encourages ownership of one's healing journey by emphasizing active participation and decision-making. This empowerment fosters confidence in managing emotional triggers, reinforcing the belief that progress is aĖainable. Each adjustment made to the plan symbolizes growth and deepened understanding, contributing positively to the overall recovery process.

Utilizing cognitive restructuring techniques can further complement the structured plan. By transforming negative thought patterns associated with triggers, individuals can shift their perceptions and reduce the power of emotional responses. This approach involves challenging unhelpful beliefs and reframing them in more balanced, constructive ways. For instance, replacing thoughts of helplessness with affirmations of strength and resilience can promote a healthier internal dialogue. With practice, cognitive restructuring can decrease the intensity of emotional triggers, enabling individuals to face them with increased confidence.

That's where the transformative impact of reshaping perceptions becomes evident. Changing how one interprets triggers alters the emotional narrative surrounding them, turning fear into opportunity for growth. Over time, this method cultivates a mindset oriented towards healing, gradually weakening the hold that triggers have had. Ultimately, incorporating guidelines and frameworks within a structured plan empowers individuals to take control of their emotional health, paving the way toward recovery.

Cognitive Restructuring

In the journey of managing Complex PTSD, reframing negative thoughts triggered by various emotional stimuli plays a crucial role in healing and growth. The essence of this approach lies in transforming these thoughts into positive affirmations, which gradually diminishes the influence that emotional triggers hold over individuals.

To begin with, this transformation process helps in reducing the power of triggers and fostering greater confidence. When individuals encounter experiences or memories that ignite distress, their initial thoughts might be dominated by negativity, fear, or helplessness. By deliberately replacing such negative thoughts with positive affirmations, individuals can disrupt the automatic response mechanism that often hinders emotional regulation. For instance, instead of believing "I cannot handle this," one can affirm "I have the strength to overcome challenges." Such affirmations not only reduce stress responses but also empower individuals to confront situations with renewed self-belief.

Moreover, adopting this technique encourages a growth mindset, which is essential for cultivating resilience. A growth mindset revolves around the belief that one's abilities and understanding can develop over time through effort, learning, and persistence. In the context of reframing thoughts, it denotes an openness to perceive difficulties as opportunities for learning rather than insurmountable obstacles. This shift in perspective facilitates resilience because individuals are more likely to persevere in the face of adversity when they view setbacks as temporary and surmountable. Emphasizing a belief such as "Every challenge is a chance to learn and grow" allows individuals to navigate their recovery with patience and optimism.

Positivity also plays a pivotal role in promoting emotional healing and supporting internal dialogue. When individuals actively cultivate positive thoughts, they engage in what can be termed as supportive self-talk. This discourse fosters a nurturing internal environment where self-compassion can thrive. Cognitive restructuring, a key component of this process, involves identifying and challenging distorted cognitions. By doing so, individuals replace self-critical or defeatist narratives with affirmations that underline their inherent worth and capabilities. For example, substituting "I am broken beyond repair" with "I am healing step by step every day" reinforces a focus on gradual progress and personal value, which is integral to healing. Furthermore, shifting perception through cognitive restructuring aids recovery significantly. Cognitive restructuring refers to an intentional change in how one perceives and interprets events and situations. For those dealing with Complex PTSD, triggers often evoke deep-seated perceptions rooted in past traumas. By consciously altering these perceptions, individuals can alter their emotional responses. This often starts by recognizing irrational thoughts or beliefs that contribute to emotional distress. Replacing these with rational, balanced thoughts not only alleviates psychological tension but also rewires the brain gradually to adapt to healthier thinking paĖerns. This foundational change in cognition becomes instrumental in long-term recovery and emotional stability.

As readers learn to reframe negative thoughts through positive affirmations, it becomes clear that the art of cognitive reframing is not merely about thinking differently but evolving one's entire mental framework. It's about establishing a foundation where resilience, healing, and positivity are interwoven into the everyday fabric of life. By integrating positive affirmations into their daily routine, individuals can create a robust defense mechanism against the inevitable encounters with emotional triggers. Reinforcing affirmations like "I am capable of navigating my emotions" or "With time, I grow stronger each day" can become powerful allies in the quest for emotional equilibrium.

Rewriting Your Narrative

Rewriting your narrative is an essential part of healing from Complex PTSD. Often, the stories we tell ourselves about who we are and what we've experienced are steeped in negativity, overshadowing our strengths and potential for recovery. Shifting this perspective can open the door to a more positive view of oneself—a transformation that is both empowering and healing. In this chapter, we venture into the practice of therapeutic writing as a tool for reshaping these self-narratives. The act of putting pen to paper allows one to explore personal experiences with honesty and without judgment, creating a space where negative perceptions can be identified, challenged, and reframed.

Therapeutic Writing Exercises

Exploring personal narratives and the potential for healing in our understanding of self can be a powerful journey. One of the most effective methods to initiate this transformation is through therapeutic writing exercises. Engaging in therapeutic writing offers individuals with Complex PTSD an avenue to examine, confront, and ultimately reshape their inner stories.

Free writing is the first step that encourages you to pour thoughts onto paper without judgment or restraint. This process taps into your subconscious, allowing hidden emotions and themes to emerge. By writing without censorship, you release inhibitions and uncover underlying patterns in your thoughts and feelings. This form of radical honesty is crucial for identifying negative perspectives that are ingrained in one's narrative. Once visible, these themes can be reframed into empowering stories. For those new to free writing, begin by seEing aside a few minutes each day to write whatever comes to mind, without worrying about structure or grammar. The key here is consistency and openness, which gradually lead to clarity and insight.

Equally significant are journaling prompts, which provide guided reflection to delve deeper into specific aspects of one's past. Structured prompts can serve as safe entry points into exploring difficult memories, helping manage the overwhelming nature of such introspection. For example, prompts might ask you to recount a moment of resilience in your life, or to describe how you overcame a particular challenge. By focusing on these narratives, you not only engage with past traumas but also highlight instances of personal strength and endurance. This shift in focus from pain to resilience fosters a more balanced perspective on one's experiences. Regularly incorporating journaling prompts into your routine creates a narrative progression where themes of growth and recovery take center stage.

LeEer writing, on the other hand, offers a unique opportunity to address unresolved emotional conflicts. Whether writing to a person, a younger version of yourself, or even abstract concepts like fear or anxiety, leEers create a structured space to articulate feelings that are often difficult to express verbally. Crafting a leEer allows for an exploration of gratitude and forgiveness, both integral to cultivating self-compassion. In addressing grievances and expressing unvoiced emotions, you open up possibilities for resolution and closure. Consider starting with a letter to someone who played a significant role in your life, thanking them for any lessons learned, even if they were painful. This practice not only helps clarify lingering emotions but also promotes healing by acknowledging the complexities of interpersonal relationships.

Storytelling techniques, particularly the use of metaphors, help visualize personal transformations and recognize the inherent strength within these journeys. Storytelling empowers you to view your life through a narrative lens, framing struggles and triumphs as parts of a greater saga. Using metaphors, such as comparing one's journey to that of a caterpillar transforming into a buẸerfly, can illustrate the growth and change experienced over time. This practice aids in recognizing agency and strength, allowing you to see setbacks not as failures but as vital stepping stones toward empowerment. Immersing oneself in storytelling reshapes perception, positioning you as the hero of your own story—a powerful and necessary shift in self-perception.

Guidelines for employing these writing strategies include creating a dedicated and distraction-free environment to explore these exercises at your own pace. Establishing a regular writing schedule can further enhance the impact of these practices, fostering a routine that supports ongoing reflection and growth. Allow yourself the flexibility to adapt these exercises to your personal style and comfort level, ensuring that the process feels authentic and meaningful.

Understanding Resilience

Exploring resilience in narrative transformation is a crucial step for individuals recovering from Complex PTSD. Resilience, at its core, is about more than just surviving difficult times; it's the ability to adapt and grow positively after facing adversity. This growth isn't merely enduring life's trials but thriving beyond them. By understanding and embracing resilience, individuals can shift their negative self-perceptions into empowering personal narratives.

Misconceptions about resilience often portray it as an inherent trait, something you're either born with or without. However, this belief overlooks the truth that resilience is not fixed; it is a skill that can be cultivated through intentional practice. Just as a muscle grows stronger with regular exercise, so too does resilience develop with mindful effort. Practices such as mindfulness, seeking support, and engaging in reflective activities can nurture resilience over time. For those living with Complex PTSD, realizing that resilience can be learned and strengthened provides hope and a tangible path toward healing.

Narrative resilience offers a profound way of rewriting our life stories to focus on growth and recovery. It's an approach deeply supported by research, suggesting that the way we interpret past experiences significantly impacts our psychological and emotional health. By consciously shifting how we tell our stories, we can highlight moments of strength and perseverance, reinforcing positive identities. This doesn't mean ignoring trauma or glossing over challenges but instead finding the threads of resilience woven throughout our histories and bringing them to the forefront.

Community support plays a vital role in fostering resilience and transforming narratives. Sharing stories within trusted circles not only alleviates the burden of isolation but also reinforces feelings of belonging and shared humanity. In environments where stories are exchanged, individuals can witness others' journeys and draw inspiration from their resilience. It becomes a collaborative effort, where each person contributes to the collective healing process. Being part of a supportive community allows for mutual empowerment, enhancing each individual's resilience and emotional well-being.

The transformative power of community lies in its ability to validate diverse experiences and provide a safe space for expression. When people share their stories, they often find commonalities that foster connections and build solidarity against the adversities faced. This sense of belonging is particularly comforting for those with Complex PTSD, as it counteracts feelings of alienation that often accompany trauma. Engaging actively in these communities not only fortifies personal resilience but also strengthens communal bonds, creating an environment where healing is truly possible.

Practices for Building Resilience

In our journey through life, resilience is akin to a sturdy vessel navigating turbulent waters. For those diagnosed with Complex PTSD, enhancing resilience becomes an essential compass for the path toward recovery. Introducing techniques and habits that fortify this crucial quality is not just beneficial, but transformative.

One of the foundational pillars in building resilience is mindfulness and grounding techniques. Mindfulness encourages an awareness of the present moment, channeling emotions positively and fostering emotional stability. Simple practices like mindful breathing or body scanning can create a mental space to process thoughts without judgment. Grounding techniques, such as focusing on sensory details like the texture of an object or the sounds around you, help anchor the mind during overwhelming moments. By cultivating these habits, individuals develop a protective shield against stressors, allowing them to recover more swiftly from emotional setbacks.

Establishing a routine enriched with self-care activities further solidifies resilience through consistent practice. Self-care is often misconceived as an occasional indulgence, yet when integrated into daily routines, it becomes a powerful tool for enduring strength. Activities like regular exercise, healthy eating, or even quiet time for hobbies contribute significantly to overall well-being. It's about creating a balance that caters to physical, emotional, and mental health necessities, thereby reinforcing resilience as a habitual layer of armor. Gentle yoga sessions or calming baths can become small rituals of renewal, promoting steady progress over time.

Another effective strategy is seÉing small, aÉainable goals, celebrating each step forward no maÉer how minor it may seem. These incremental achievements serve as milestones that mark the journey of growth and resilience. With each goal realized, confidence flourishes, and a sense of accomplishment strengthens the resolve to face future challenges. For example, goals could range from completing a short walk to engaging in social activities once a week. Celebrating these victories reinforces positive paÉerns of behavior and contributes to a resilient outlook.

Mutual support within groups sharing narratives of strength provides a different but equally vital layer of resilience-building. When individuals come together to share their stories, they create a shared tapestry of strength that benefits everyone involved. Group seÉings allow for the exchange of personal experiences, thus fostering empathy and understanding. This mutual support network acts as a reservoir of collective wisdom, where participants find reassurance and empowerment through others' journeys. For instance, peer support groups or community gatherings offer opportunities to hear diverse perspectives, which can illuminate new paths toward healing and adaptation.

These strategies, while straightforward, form a comprehensive approach to cultivating resilience. Each method interweaves with the others, forming a robust framework that sustains individuals through their recovery journey. Tailoring these practices to personal preferences and lifestyles ensures that resilience becomes a natural response rather than a forced effort.

Mindfulness and grounding lay the foundation by encouraging individuals to remain present and composed amidst distress. Consistent self-care routines provide a steady rhythm to life, nurturing an environment in which resilience can flourish naturally. Setting and achieving small goals injects positivity and momentum into daily life, reaffirming progress and potential. Lastly, embracing mutual support highlights the power of community in healing—acknowledging that sometimes, strength is found not only within us but beside us.

Role of Self-Narratives in Recovery

In the journey of healing from Complex PTSD, transforming negative self-perceptions into positive stories plays a crucial role in recovery. This transition is not just about changing how one tells their story; it fundamentally shifts how individuals understand themselves. When someone entrenched in negative self-narratives begins to see themselves in a new light—one that highlights strengths and achievements—they start fostering self-awareness and confidence. This newfound self-awareness helps people identify paĖerns in their thoughts and behaviors. Recognizing these paĖerns empowers individuals to break cycles of negativity, ultimately leading to improved mental and emotional well-being.

The process of reframing one's self-narratives involves recognizing and embracing personal strengths. These are often overshadowed by trauma but are essential for resilience. When an individual acknowledges their capacity to overcome past challenges, it contributes significantly to self-belief. This positive outlook does more than merely boost morale; it builds a solid foundation for facing future adversities. By highlighting personal strengths within their narratives, individuals learn to rely on inner resources they may not have fully appreciated before. This recognition transforms their worldview, instilling a belief that they possess the necessary tools to manage life's uncertainties.

Structured storytelling serves as a powerful technique to enhance clarity in self-exploration. It provides a framework where individuals can organize thoughts, emotions, and events coherently. This method is beneficial because it encourages introspection, allowing people to connect deeply with their personal journey. Through structured storytelling, individuals can weave together aspects of their identity that were once fragmented by trauma. This holistic view aids in understanding the entirety of their experiences, providing a sense of continuity and meaning. The clarity gained through this process is invaluable, as it offers a clearer vision of one's life path and potential directions for the future.

Furthermore, recognizing personal growth through reshaped narratives aligns closely with therapeutic outcomes and empowerment. When individuals observe the progress they've made, it reinforces their healing journey and validates their efforts towards recovery. Reshaping narratives shows that even amidst pain and struggle, there is room for growth and transformation. It shifts focus from what was lost to what has been gained. Empowerment emerges from this realization—the acknowledgment that change is possible and that individuals hold the keys to their destiny. This perspective aligns with many therapeutic approaches that emphasize patient autonomy and self-efficacy as pillars of recovery.

As individuals progress in rewriting their narratives, they also cultivate a unique form of empowerment linked to storytelling. Sharing personal stories with others, whether in therapy or support groups, fosters connection and validation. This communal aspect of narrative sharing reinforces the understanding that no one is alone in their struggles. Hearing others' journeys can inspire courage and resilience, encouraging individuals to continue exploring and revising their narratives. This mutual exchange of stories not only heals but creates a supportive network that strengthens collective resilience.

Moreover, the art of storytelling extends beyond the individual level; it impacts how society views trauma and recovery. As more people begin to share their reimagined narratives, it challenges societal stigmas associated with mental health issues. Opening dialogues about trauma and healing normalizes these conversations, creating a more empathetic and informed public. This social shift benefits everyone, as increasing awareness leads to more inclusive and supportive environments.

For those seeking to transform their narratives, starting small can be incredibly effective. Begin by identifying specific instances where positive qualities were evident, such as times of kindness, perseverance, or creativity. Integrate these moments into a broader narrative that reflects a resilient and adaptive self. Over time, this practice becomes natural, and the positive narrative theme will become the dominant storyline. This approach not only aids personal growth but prepares individuals to confront future challenges with increased strength.

Readers may wonder how to embark on this profound process of rewriting their histories. While professional guidance can be beneficial, everyday practices like journaling, meditation, or creative expression can serve as catalysts for change. Reflective exercises help in identifying core beliefs and values, guiding the creation of a narrative that genuinely represents one's essence.

Ultimately, transforming self-narratives is an ongoing journey that evolves alongside personal growth. It's important to remember that this process is not linear, nor does it have a definitive endpoint. Instead, it adapts to life's ebb and flow, offering a reliable tool for navigating the complexities of human experience. Embracing this dynamic aspect of narrative transformation allows individuals to live authentically and with renewed purpose.

Community and Shared Narratives

In the journey of healing and transformation from Complex PTSD, the role of community cannot be overstated. The simple act of sharing personal stories within supportive groups is a powerful tool that fosters a sense of belonging and nurtures resilience. By engaging in these narrative exchanges, individuals are not only validating their own experiences but also contributing to a tapestry of shared resilience. For those who have felt isolated by their experiences, being part of a community where one's story is heard and respected can offer immense relief and support.

When individuals gather to share their narratives, they contribute to a collective understanding that transcends personal trauma. This shared storytelling allows participants to see pieces of themselves reflected in others' journeys. In doing so, a network of mutual support emerges, characterized by empathy and camaraderie. Witnessing parallels in others' experiences can help dismantle feelings of isolation and nurture a sense of solidarity that is crucial in the healing process. Each story told contributes to a broader narrative of overcoming adversity, reinforcing the notion that healing is not only possible but aＥainable with community support.

Encouraging individuals to connect and exchange experiences in a safe environment strengthens community bonds and enhances mutual aid. This practice not only builds bridges between individuals but fosters a compassionate understanding of different yet relatable paths to recovery. Through conversations and shared reflections, a group becomes more than just a gathering—it transforms into a nurturing ecosystem where each member plays a vital role in bolstering the resilience of others.

Particularly in structured seＥings such as group therapy or peer-support meetings, members benefit from observing and learning from each other's coping strategies and successes. These interactions allow them to draw strength from the victories of others, fostering hope and determination in their own journeys toward recovery. The communal experience provides a mirror in which members can reflect on their progress, drawing inspiration and motivation from stories of growth and resilience.

Participating in collective narrative-sharing groups enhances resilience not just through individual storytelling, but through witnessing the strength others embody. Observing how peers navigate challenges highlights resilience as an aＥainable quality, encouraging participants to recognize similar strengths within themselves. Often, these insights gained from shared narratives spark introspection, motivating individuals to reframe their personal stories in a more positive light. Such reframing is essential for rewriting self-narratives and cultivating emotional empowerment.

The beauty of collaboration in community circles lies in the diverse perspectives and stories exchanged within these spaces. Each participant brings a unique history, perspective, and wisdom, enriching the dialogue and offering fresh insights to others. Engaging with varied viewpoints helps members to broaden their understanding of resilience, offering novel strategies and approaches to healing. This diversity empowers individuals to explore multiple pathways to recovery, ultimately leading to a richer, more nuanced understanding of personal growth.

One of the greatest gifts of community storytelling is the opportunity it provides for healing through narrative exchange. These encounters often lead to deep, meaningful discussions where members learn to appreciate the power of vulnerability. In sharing fears and triumphs alike, individuals cultivate a deeper connection with themselves and their peers, fostering an environment where healing naturally unfolds. By exchanging stories, members can challenge entrenched beliefs, recognize new ways of thinking, and acknowledge the progress they've made.

In turn, this supportive dynamic nurtures a culture of resilience, where the focus extends beyond mere survival to thriving despite adversity. Participating in such communities enables individuals to draw upon collective strength, reinforcing their resilience and capacity to overcome future challenges. Members find encouragement in knowing they are not alone, buÉressed by the wisdom and support of their peers as they continue their journey towards inner peace.

Understanding Trauma's Impact on Relationships

Trauma's impact on relationships is profound, often weaving a complex web of behaviors and emotions that affect how individuals relate to themselves and others. The invisible scars left by trauma can manifest in various ways, such as altered perceptions, communication barriers, and emotional defenses. Recognizing these patterns is crucial to understanding how trauma reshapes interpersonal dynamics. Every person carries their unique history into relationships, but for those with Complex PTSD, past experiences can cast long shadows over their present interactions. By delving into these relational challenges, this chapter begins the journey of uncovering the intricate connections between trauma and relationship difficulties.

Identifying Unhealthy Relationship Patterns

Recognizing the patterns that trauma imprints on relationships is a critical step toward fostering healthier connections. Trauma, particularly complex trauma, can significantly alter how individuals engage with others, often manifesting in ways that hinder the formation of deep, meaningful relationships. One of the most prominent consequences of trauma is distrust, which erects barriers, leaving little room for authentic connection.

Distrust, stemming from past wounds, tends to create invisible walls between individuals. This barrier can be so subtle that it often goes unnoticed until it significantly impacts interpersonal relationships. People who have experienced trauma might continually question the motives and intentions of those around them, making it difficult to establish trust. This skepticism doesn't only affect personal relationships but can extend to professional and social settings as well. As a result, opportunities for genuine interaction are missed, isolating individuals even further. It becomes essential, then, to recognize these patterns early, allowing for intervention that fosters openness and vulnerability when appropriate.

Another common pattern resulting from trauma is a fear of intimacy. This fear acts as a protective mechanism but also deprives individuals of emotional satisfaction and fulfillment. Trauma survivors might struggle with letting others get too close, fearing exposure or rejection. Intimacy requires vulnerability, something that trauma has taught many to avoid at all costs. The paradox lies in the desire for connection yet feeling trapped by the very mechanisms put in place for self-protection. Breaking free from this cycle involves acknowledging the fear and gradually allowing oneself to experience closeness with trusted others.

Codependency is another unhealthy pattern that often arises from past trauma. When individuals feel overly responsible for the emotions and well-being of others, they may slip into codependent dynamics. This might present as an intense need to please others or an inability to assert one's own needs and desires. In such relationships, boundaries become blurred, and personal identity may be lost. The roots of codependency often lie in early experiences where individuals were conditioned to prioritize others' needs over their own. Recognizing these tendencies is crucial; awareness can pave the way for developing healthier relational habits where mutual respect and individuality are valued.

Avoiding conflict is another prevalent issue for trauma survivors, leading to unresolved issues and growing resentment over time. Conflict, although uncomfortable, is a natural part of relationships. However, for someone with a history of trauma, confronting disagreements can trigger memories of past hurts or fears of abandonment. To protect themselves, they might choose avoidance over confrontation. While this approach might provide immediate relief, it ultimately results in accumulated tensions and unmet needs. Learning to engage in constructive conflict resolution is vital. It involves understanding that disagreements can coexist with care and love and need not threaten relationship stability.

The journey to recognizing and overcoming these patterns is neither quick nor easy, yet it is essential for healing. One practical guideline for rebuilding trust involves beginning with small steps. Sharing minor vulnerabilities and observing reactions can build confidence over time, as each positive interaction reinforces the possibility of safety in relationships. Supporting someone in this process requires patience and empathy, recognizing that each step taken towards trust and connection is significant.

Engaging in therapy or support groups can be beneficial, providing safe spaces to explore these patterns more deeply. Therapy can offer insights into why certain behaviors persist, equip individuals with tools to alter these patterns, and provide a supportive environment for practicing new, healthier relationship dynamics. Friends and family can play a pivotal role by offering understanding and avoiding judgment, reinforcing the message that everyone deserves healthy, supportive connections.

Role of Trust Issues

Trust forms the foundation of any healthy relationship, yet for those experiencing complex trauma, trust can often feel elusive, casting shadows on attachments. Trauma not only alters an individual's emotional landscape but also skews how they perceive others' intentions. Those grappling with past trauma might find themselves questioning the motives behind even the kindest gestures. This persistent doubt serves as a defense mechanism, rooted in fear and previous experiences of betrayal or harm.

As a result, behaviors and words that are harmless or well-meaning could be interpreted as malicious or threatening.

Such distorted perceptions create barriers to forming genuine connections. Individuals may become overly guarded, anticipating pain before it occurs. This anticipation, born from deep-seated distrust, leads to missed opportunities in relationships. For instance, rejecting a friend's invitation due to fears of being judged or abandoned can prevent nurturing what might have blossomed into a supportive relationship. The cycle of expectation and avoidance becomes self-fulfilling, as distrust confirms its own validity when potential connections falter under the weight of suspicion.

To break this cycle and rebuild trust, individuals must first acknowledge their skewed perceptions and work towards altering them. Techniques such as open communication and mindfulness can be transformative. Engaging in dialogues where both parties express feelings and intentions can slowly dismantle the walls constructed by mistrust. Mindfulness, on the other hand, helps individuals stay grounded in the present, reducing the tendency to project past traumas onto current interactions. By focusing on the here and now, the overwhelming influence of history diminishes, paving the way for new perceptions.

Furthermore, therapy plays a crucial role in rebuilding trust. Working with a mental health professional provides individuals with a safe space to explore their fears and impulses while learning new coping mechanisms. Therapists can guide conversations around trust and bring aÉention to subconscious paÉerns that hinder relationships. Cognitive-behavioral approaches, for example, help modify negative thought paÉerns and promote more balanced ways of thinking about relationships.

Beyond individual efforts, fostering secure aÉachments necessitates strategies that involve mutual engagement. Creating environments where vulnerability is met with empathy rather than judgment encourages openness. In relationships, it's essential to prioritize consistency and reliability, as these reinforce the sense of security. When actions align with words repeatedly over time, trust grows naturally.

Another critical strategy involves seEing realistic expectations. Many people emerging from traumatic experiences hold others to impossible standards, hoping for immediate proof of trustworthiness. However, trust is a gradual process; expecting instant perfection can set relationships up for failure. Acknowledging human imperfections and allowing room for mistakes fosters a more forgiving and understanding dynamic.

Empathy serves as a bridge for establishing secure attachments. AEempts at understanding a partner's or friend's perspective, especially during conflicts, demonstrate willingness to embrace complexity rather than retreating into defensiveness. This practice can significantly reduce misunderstandings fueled by trauma-induced assumptions.

Additionally, constructing rituals or intentional moments strengthens bonds and enhances aEachment security. These could be as simple as regular check-ins or shared activities, which cultivate familiarity and reinforce a sense of belonging. Rituals provide predictability and continuity amidst the chaos of healing, underscoring the commitment to the relationship.

Fear of Intimacy

Trauma often leaves deep emotional scars that shape how individuals perceive and interact with the world around them. One of the significant impacts of trauma is the avoidance of close relationships, a behavior that can stifle emotional satisfaction and fulfillment. For those diagnosed with Complex PTSD, this avoidance can become a familiar, yet isolating, paEern in their lives.

Fear of intimacy is not uncommon among those who have experienced trauma. It manifests as an instinctive withdrawal from situations that invite closeness, whether emotional or physical. This fear is rooted in the need for self-preservation, as past experiences might have taught these individuals that vulnerability equates to harm or betrayal. Consequently, they may build walls around themselves, consciously or unconsciously avoiding situations that require opening up to another person. This protective mechanism, while serving an immediate purpose, can lead to long-term repercussions, such as feelings of loneliness and unfulfilled emotional needs.

Everyday examples of avoidance are revealing. Consider someone who has experienced trauma in a previous relationship; they might shy away from dating altogether or keep potential partners at arm's length. In friendships, they may avoid deep conversations or fail to acknowledge shared emotions, thus preventing connections from deepening. At work, the same person might refrain from team activities or social gatherings, fearing judgment or exposure.

For others, avoidance might look like being overly critical of those who try to get close or engaging in self-sabotaging behaviors when relationships start to develop. These actions are often subconscious attempts to push others away before they have a chance to hurt—despite the possible joy and support those relationships could bring. The cumulative effect of these avoidance strategies is a life that feels safe but hollow, lacking the warmth and interaction that make life truly vibrant and meaningful.

Constructive techniques for overcoming this fear involve a multi-faceted approach. Acknowledging the fear is the first step, recognizing it as a learned response rather than an inherent trait. Individuals are encouraged to engage in self-reflection, possibly through journaling, to trace the origins of their fears and understand how these fears manifest in their daily interactions.

Gradual exposure to feared scenarios can also be beneficial. This might involve setting small, manageable goals, such as having deeper conversations with friends or gradually participating more in groups. Each successful interaction serves to reinforce the idea that intimacy does not necessarily lead to pain, helping to rewrite old narratives with new, positive experiences. Support networks, both personal and professional, play a crucial role here, offering encouragement and understanding as individuals navigate these challenging waters.

Therapy provides a safe and structured environment to address intimacy fears directly. Here, individuals can explore their past experiences and learn how these have shaped their current behaviors. Therapeutic techniques such as cognitive-behavioral therapy (CBT) can be instrumental in identifying and challenging negative thought paÈerns, replacing them with healthier beliefs about oneself and others. Additionally, therapists can guide clients through exercises that help desensitize them to closeness, fostering a sense of security in intimate situations.

The role of therapy extends beyond addressing fear; it is pivotal in rebuilding trust within relationships. Trust is fundamental for intimacy, yet it is often shaÈered by trauma. Through therapy, individuals can learn to trust themselves and their judgment again, which in turn helps them extend trust to others. This process is gradual and requires patience, but it lays the foundation for more fulfilling relationships.

Furthermore, therapy highlights the importance of boundaries as a tool for managing intimacy. SeÈing clear boundaries allows individuals to feel safe while opening up, creating a balance between self-protection and connection. Knowing one's limits and communicating them effectively can prevent feeling overwhelmed and ensure that both parties in a relationship feel respected and understood.

For mental health professionals, understanding the complexity of intimacy fears is essential for effective intervention. They must approach each case with empathy, tailoring therapeutic strategies to the unique needs and histories of their clients. By maintaining a supportive and non-judgmental stance, therapists can empower their clients to explore and challenge their fears, facilitating healing and growth.

Friends and family members of those with trauma histories also play a vital role. Their willingness to be patient and understanding can significantly reduce the pressure on individuals with trauma to rush into intimacy. Simple acts of kindness, consistency, and genuine aÈempts to understand can bridge gaps that avoidance creates, showing that love and acceptance do not always come with conditions.

Codependency and Control

Delving into the intricate world of trauma's impact on relationships, it becomes imperative to explore behaviors intricately linked to control and codependency. At the heart of such dynamics are codependent traits, which often have deep roots embedded in past traumas. Codependency typically manifests as an excessive reliance on others for approval and identity, often blurring personal boundaries. It is characterized by enabling behavior, where individuals might feel compelled to fix or rescue others, sometimes at the expense of their own well-being.

From a psychological standpoint, codependency can be seen as a byproduct of unresolved trauma. Traumatic experiences can warp self-perception and foster internalized beliefs that one's value is inherently tied to another's happiness. For those with Complex PTSD, these tendencies might stem from caretaking roles assumed in unpredictable environments during formative years, leading to adulthood paÈerns where one feels more comfortable giving than receiving. Recognizing these traits is crucial, as they pose significant barriers to forming mutually satisfying relationships.

Equally concerning within trauma-impacted relationships are controlling dynamics. Control may arise as a means of coping with feelings of vulnerability. For someone who has experienced trauma, maintaining control can create an illusion of safety amidst chaos. However, this need for control might manifest in ways that stifle both parties involved—be it through micromanaging daily activities, dictating emotional responses, or establishing rigid relationship rules. Such behaviors can inadvertently push loved ones away, fueling resentment and a lack of genuine connection.

Understanding how these behaviors develop requires a nuanced analysis of past events and subsequent belief systems. Often, controlling dynamics emerge from a fear-based response to loss, rejection, or betrayal experienced during traumatic episodes. The mind learns to anticipate threats, real or perceived, and seeks to mitigate risk by exerting authority over one's environment, including interpersonal relations. This mechanism, while protective in nature, often leads to unintended consequences, perpetuating cycles of dysfunction.

To unlearn these detrimental habits and foster healthier relational patterns, practical exercises can prove beneficial. One effective exercise involves practicing mindfulness to cultivate awareness of one's thoughts and actions in real-time. By observing moments when control or codependency tendencies arise, individuals can pause and reflect rather than react impulsively. Journaling is also an invaluable tool—it allows for the exploration of emotions and identification of recurring themes that contribute to unhealthy behaviors.

Another practical approach includes setting small, achievable goals aimed at fostering independence. Engaging in hobbies or social activities independently encourages personal growth and reduces reliance on others for validation. Additionally, communication exercises, such as active listening and expressing needs assertively without guilt, help redefine interaction patterns, gradually shifting them towards equality and respect.

Furthermore, engaging with therapeutic interventions, such as cognitive-behavioral therapy (CBT) or dialectical behavior therapy (DBT), offers structured opportunities to challenge ingrained beliefs and replace them with healthier alternatives. In CBT, individuals learn to identify and modify distorted thought paĖerns, while DBT emphasizes emotion regulation and distress tolerance—both vital for breaking free from control and codependency cycles.

Steps to Establish Healthy Boundaries

Navigating the realm of relationships after experiencing trauma can be daunting. SeĖing boundaries becomes a pivotal step toward nurturing healthier dynamics and safeguarding one's well-being. Boundaries serve as the invisible lines that define personal limits and expectations in interactions with others. They are essential for protecting oneself from further harm and creating a space where healing can begin to take root.

To establish these boundaries, self-reflection serves as a foundational practice. It involves delving into one's thoughts and emotions to discern what feels comfortable and what triggers discomfort or distress. Self-reflection encourages individuals to pause and assess their needs, desires, and vulnerabilities. Through this introspection, one gains clarity on personal limits— those things that they are willing and unwilling to tolerate in relationships. For instance, someone might realize they need time alone regularly to recharge or discover that criticisms about certain sensitive topics are a no-go zone for them.

Once personal limits are identified, communicating these boundaries effectively becomes crucial. Communication is the bridge that allows others to understand where you stand. This means clearly articulating your needs and expectations without ambiguity. For example, when expressing the need for personal space, one might say, "I need some quiet time each evening to unwind and reflect." This kind of straightforward statement helps prevent misunderstandings and paves the way for others to respect individual preferences. Effective communication also involves listening actively to the responses of others. Engaging in these dialogues fosters mutual understanding and empathy, as both parties gain insights into each other's worldviews. Open discussions about boundaries create an environment where people feel heard and validated, encouraging them to honor these limits willingly.

Enforcing boundaries consistently is another critical component in this journey. SeÈing boundaries is not enough; they must be respected to be meaningful. This calls for a commitment to reinforce these limits whenever they are overlooked or violated. For example, if someone continuously interrupts during conversations despite requests for them to stop, it becomes necessary to remind them of this boundary and assert its importance. Consistency in enforcing boundaries signals seriousness and determination in maintaining one's well-being and autonomy. However, consistent enforcement does not imply rigidity. Life is dynamic, and so are relationships. Boundaries may need to evolve over time. What felt right in one phase of life might need adjustment later on. Regular reevaluation of boundaries ensures they remain relevant and supportive of current relationship dynamics. This process involves checking in with oneself periodically to assess whether existing boundaries still serve their intended purpose or require modification. Perhaps a boundary around sharing personal stories shifts as trust deepens or new experiences ensue.

Guidelines for seÈing and maintaining boundaries post-trauma can prove invaluable in navigating these complexities. Begin by dedicating time to self-reflection regularly, perhaps through journaling or meditation, to identify your personal limits. When ready to communicate boundaries, approach these conversations with openness and clarity, fostering understanding rather than confrontation. Practice assertiveness, emphasizing your needs, and be prepared to reinforce your boundaries patiently but firmly when necessary. Remember the importance of flexibility, allowing your boundaries to adapt as your relationships and circumstances evolve.

Healing Through Self-Empowerment

Healing through self-empowerment is an exploration of the profound journey toward personal transformation, particularly for those grappling with Complex PTSD. When navigating the aftermath of trauma, individuals often find that their sense of control and autonomy has been diminished. This chapter delves into the empowering practices that can restore this lost agency, offering a pathway to reclaim one's life and narrative. By focusing on nurturing inner strength and fostering growth, the chapter encourages readers to see themselves as capable of overcoming the lingering shadows of past experiences.

Practices that Promote Autonomy

Autonomy is the cornerstone of self-empowerment, particularly when it comes to healing from trauma like Complex PTSD. At its core, autonomy means taking ownership of one's life and decisions—something that trauma can often strip away. When individuals experience complex trauma, they may feel as though their sense of self and ability to direct their own lives have been compromised. Rebuilding this sense of autonomy becomes critical for genuine healing because it empowers individuals to reclaim control over their narrative and circumstances.

Understanding the role of autonomy in recovery is a fundamental concept. Trauma survivors often grapple with feelings of powerlessness and a lack of control, but understanding that reclaiming control over life is essential for overcoming traumatic effects begins the healing journey. By learning to make choices that align with personal values and needs, individuals start to dismantle the influence of past traumas on their present life. This is not merely about making choices, but also about recognizing one's inherent worth and right to decide the course of one's life. For many, small steps such as deciding how to spend their time or setting preferences in daily routines contribute significantly to re-establishing control.

Establishing personal boundaries plays a vital role in fostering autonomy and protecting emotional space. Boundaries are essential for maintaining mental well-being as they create a safe environment where one can grow and heal. SeEing personal boundaries might involve expressing one's needs, saying no when necessary, or even limiting exposure to situations that could trigger stress or anxiety. These boundaries help distinguish between what is acceptable and unacceptable, allowing individuals to protect their mental spaces from potential harm. As individuals with Complex PTSD learn to assert their boundaries, they begin to nurture a sense of safety and respect, crucial for emotional recovery. Moreover, these boundaries serve as a form of self-care, reminding individuals of the importance of looking after both their physical and emotional selves.

Personal agency is closely tied to decision-making skills, which foster both self-determination and autonomy. When individuals build their decision-making abilities, they enhance their sense of personal agency. Decision-making allows individuals to exercise control consciously, reinforcing their ability to shape their reality according to their preferences and goals. In the context of recovery, decision-making is not just about choosing between options but involves reflecting on what truly resonates with their inner selves. Developing these skills empowers individuals to make thoughtful and deliberate choices aligning with their values and aspirations, further promoting healing and growth.

To appreciate this inherent ability fully, it's important for readers to embrace an empowering mindset. Empowerment practices encourage individuals to acknowledge and accept their capabilities, thus fostering an optimistic outlook on the recovery process. Consider empowerment as a gradual unfolding rather than a sudden transformation. Every positive choice made, boundary set, or decision taken is evidence of growing strength and resilience. People come to recognize themselves as active participants in crafting their future rather than passive recipients of their circumstances.

Incorporating empowerment practices into daily life can be transformative. For instance, seEing achievable goals, whether small or significant, provides individuals with direction and motivation. These goals act as signposts along the path of recovery, offering reassurance and measurable progress. Furthermore, engaging in activities that reinforce agency—such as volunteering, creative pursuits, or joining supportive communities—can bolster confidence and affirm one's capacity to impact the world constructively.

The journey towards self-empowerment through autonomy requires patience and persistence. It is not a path devoid of challenges, but each obstacle overcome represents a victory in itself. Even setbacks hold lessons that contribute to the overarching narrative of growth and healing. Practicing mindfulness or journaling can aid in processing these experiences, enabling individuals to reflect on their journey, celebrate their progress, and recalibrate when necessary.

Empowering practices have far-reaching benefits beyond the individual, affecting relationships and social dynamics. As individuals grow more confident in their autonomous selves, they become beEer equipped to engage with others transparently and authentically. This, in turn, fosters healthier connections characterized by mutual respect and understanding. The ripple effect of empowerment extends to friends and family, who witness firsthand the transformative resilience developed through autonomy and empowerment.

Support networks play an invaluable role in reinforcing empowerment. Friends, family, and mental health professionals provide encouragement, guidance, and validation. They serve as sounding boards, helping individuals navigate challenging decisions while respecting their autonomy. Mental health professionals, especially, offer tailored strategies to cultivate autonomy, ensuring that therapeutic interventions support clients' innate strengths and objectives.

Establishing Personal Boundaries

Establishing healthy boundaries is a fundamental step in fostering self-empowerment and healing for individuals dealing with Complex PTSD. By defining and maintaining these boundaries, individuals can create a protective and nurturing environment that supports both emotional safety and autonomy.

Firstly, it's crucial to understand how healthy boundaries play a role in preventing emotional overwhelm. For those navigating the intricate landscape of Complex PTSD, emotions can often feel like a turbulent storm, threatening to sweep them away. Boundaries act as an anchor amidst this chaos, providing stability and clarity. By establishing clear limits, one can manage emotional stimuli more effectively, reducing the risk of becoming overwhelmed and creating space for mental well-being. This process involves recognizing personal capacities and understanding when to step back from situations or interactions that may drain emotional energy.

Defining personal limits also plays a critical role in reinforcing self-respect. When individuals set boundaries, they are essentially communicating their needs and values to others and, importantly, to themselves. This communication serves as a powerful affirmation of self-worth. Imagine a scenario where someone consistently finds themselves feeling exhausted after social gatherings but continues to aEend them out of obligation. By seEing a boundary, such as deciding to leave early or participate selectively, they are honoring their own needs. This strengthens self-respect and fosters a sense of safety in relationships, as others begin to understand and respect these limits as well.

Moreover, effective boundary-seEing nurtures relationships and enhances self-worth. Contrary to the misconception that boundaries create distance, they actually foster deeper connections by establishing mutual respect and understanding. When individuals communicate their limits clearly, they teach others how to engage with them supportively and respectfully. This not only protects personal well-being but also encourages healthier dynamics in interpersonal relationships. In essence, boundaries serve as guidelines for how we wish to be treated, promoting a nurturing environment where genuine connections can flourish.

An empowering aspect of boundary establishment is the opportunity it provides for advocacy and communication. Learning to advocate for oneself is vital in promoting agency, especially for those who have experienced trauma. Advocacy involves expressing one's needs and desires assertively yet respectfully. It is about voicing personal truths and ensuring they are heard and considered. For instance, an individual may need to articulate their need for alone time to recharge emotionally, despite social expectations. By doing so, they exercise agency over their life decisions and interactions, enhancing their overall sense of empowerment.

As individuals embark on the journey of seÈing healthy boundaries, it is essential to offer practical guidance to navigate this transformative process smoothly. Establishing personal boundaries demands introspection and courage. Ask yourself what truly maÈers, what drains you, and what sustains you. These reflections help define your boundaries. Begin by identifying areas in your life where you feel discomfort or resentment, as these feelings often signal boundary violations. Once identified, assert these boundaries clearly and consistently in your interactions, remembering that they are a reflection of your needs and deserve respect.

SeÈing these boundaries prevents emotional overwhelm, enabling individuals to focus on their healing process without being inundated by external pressures. Clear, consistent communication of these boundaries, whether it's saying no to additional commitments or requesting space when needed, is key to maintaining emotional equilibrium. By navigating this process with empathy and clarity, both for oneself and others involved, individuals can effectively prevent the emotional overloads that often accompany complex trauma responses.

Additionally, defining personal limits plays a dual role. It extends beyond self-respect to encompass an element of self-care, a critical component for anyone dealing with Complex PTSD. As individuals articulate their limits, they practice self-compassion, acknowledging their right to prioritize their well-being. This creates a ripple effect in their relationships. Partners, friends, and family start recognizing and valuing these boundaries, fostering a secure environment where individuals feel respected and valued. The result is a nurturing relationship built on authentic engagement rather than obligatory interaction.

In protecting one's self-worth and nurturing relationships, boundary seEing must be seen as an ongoing practice, adaptable as circumstances evolve. Boundaries are not static rules but dynamic elements of personal wellness strategies. They require regular assessment and realignment to ensure they continue to serve their protective and nurturing purposes effectively. Open dialogue with trusted allies can further enhance this process, inviting supportive feedback while maintaining control over one's narrative.

Finally, effective boundary seEing necessitates embracing and celebrating one's ability to advocate for themselves. Self-advocacy involves confidently expressing one's boundaries and enforcing them with consistency. It underscores the importance of not just seEing boundaries but also upholding them through assertive communication. Whether it involves straightforward conversations or gentle reminders, advocating for boundaries promotes agency, allowing individuals to reclaim power lost to past traumas.

Building Decision-Making Skills

In our journey toward healing through self-empowerment, recognizing the role of decision-making can be transformative. Complex PTSD often leaves individuals feeling like control has slipped from their grasp, and regaining that sense of agency is crucial. Making thoughtful and deliberate decisions helps align actions with personal values and well-being, fostering a sense of control. When choices reflect what maÉers most to an individual, it reinforces their intrinsic values, promoting emotional stability and resilience.

Consider, for example, a person deciding to pursue a new hobby. The decision isn't just about the activity itself; it's also about prioritizing joy and fulfillment. By consciously choosing something that resonates with their interests and values, they create positive experiences that counterbalance past trauma. This practice continually invites introspection and authenticity into everyday life.

Exploring choices further enhances personal growth and expression. It broadens perspectives and encourages stepping outside of comfort zones. This exploration is not just about making monumental changes but appreciating small, meaningful shifts in everyday life. For instance, trying a different route on a daily walk or experimenting with a new recipe can bring a sense of novelty and rejuvenation.

Each choice represents an opportunity to stretch cognitive and emotional boundaries, allowing individuals to discover new facets of themselves. As this exploration progresses, it fosters a deeper understanding of personal preferences, likes, and dislikes, ultimately contributing to a stronger sense of self. This empowerment allows for more informed, confident decisions in the future.

Reflecting on past decisions provides another layer of insight into one's behavior and thought patterns. Looking back at previous choices reveals paĖerns, successes, and areas for improvement. This reflection process is constructive, offering a learning experience that informs future decision-making. It's similar to reviewing a play in sports to identify what worked and what didn't—informing strategies moving forward.

By identifying recurring themes in past decisions, individuals can recognize triggers and areas requiring change. This self-awareness is empowering, as it illuminates pathways for growth and transformation. Moreover, acknowledging past triumphs bolsters confidence, reinforcing the belief that one is capable of making sound decisions even amidst adversity.

Self-advocacy strategies are integral to articulating one's needs and preferences effectively. Empowered communication means clearly expressing desires, boundaries, and limitations. These skills are essential for both personal interactions and navigating professional environments. Consider crafting assertive statements that respect both oneself and others. This clarity in communication prevents misunderstandings, nurtures relationships, and promotes mutual respect.

For instance, when discussing therapeutic goals with a counselor, practicing self-advocacy ensures that individual needs are prioritized in the healing process. It fosters collaboration, where both client and therapist work together toward shared objectives. Outside therapy, self-advocacy might involve requesting flexible arrangements at work to accommodate mental health needs, demonstrating the practical application of these strategies in everyday life.

Developing decision-making skills goes beyond immediate choices, emphasizing the necessity of seĖing realistic goals and evaluating options carefully. Engaging in activities like journaling or discussing decisions with trusted peers can facilitate this process, providing diverse perspectives and feedback that enrich decision-making abilities.

Guidelines can serve as a supportive framework in this skill-building, offering techniques for weighing pros and cons, considering long-term impacts, and incorporating intuition alongside logic. Such structured approaches enhance confidence, promoting responsible autonomy that aligns with overall well-being.

Setting Realistic Healing Goals

In the journey of healing from Complex PTSD, setting achievable goals plays a crucial role in aligning personal aspirations with recovery efforts. Realistic goals serve as a guiding roadmap for individuals navigating the complexities of their healing process. When overwhelmed by memories and emotions, establishing aÉainable goals can create a sense of direction and clarity. This process is not just about ticking off tasks but about crafting steps toward tangible progress, helping to restore a sense of control that trauma often disrupts.

Picture the healing process as a vast, uncharted landscape. Without a map, one could easily feel lost or overwhelmed by the terrain. Realistic goals function as this map, breaking down the overwhelming task of managing Complex PTSD into manageable, digestible steps. For instance, instead of aiming to "overcome PTSD," a more realistic goal could be "practice mindfulness for 10 minutes daily." Such specific goals are not only achievable but also prevent feelings of failure that may arise from overly ambitious expectations. Celebrating small victories along the way can build momentum and provide motivation, reinforcing a narrative of growth and resilience.

The alignment of these goals with personal values significantly enhances motivation and commitment. Understanding what maÉers most to an individual provides the fuel needed to persist through challenging times. For those dealing with Complex PTSD, where trust and self-worth might have been eroded by past experiences, rooting goals in deeply held values can reignite a sense of purpose and direction. It's like planting a seed that grows into a sturdy tree of recovery, anchored firmly by its roots. For example, if fostering relationships is a core value, a goal might involve engaging in social activities that promote connection and reduce isolation — thereby cultivating both personal growth and relational healing.

An invaluable tool in this process is the formulation of SMART goals: Specific, Measurable, Achievable, Relevant, and Time-bound. These criteria ensure that goals are clear and feasible, removing ambiguity that can lead to procrastination or anxiety. To illustrate, let's look at a practical application of a SMART goal within the context of Complex PTSD recovery. A general objective like "improve emotional regulation" becomes much more actionable when transformed into a SMART goal such as, "Practice journaling for 15 minutes every night to process emotions, and review entries weekly to track progress." This approach allows for measurable outcomes, making it easier to recognize improvements over time, no matter how small they might appear initially.

Crafting SMART goals also empowers individuals by encouraging them to take ownership of their healing journey. It invites reflection and active participation, fostering a deeper understanding of one's needs and strengths. This empowerment is especially vital for those recovering from trauma, as it helps rebuild the agency that might have been diminished. Moreover, it instills confidence in one's ability to make positive changes, transforming the recovery path into a series of intentional actions rather than passive waiting.

Celebrating milestones, even minor ones, is another pivotal aspect of maintaining motivation on this journey. Acknowledging accomplishments, regardless of size, not only reinforces motivation but also cultivates a positive self-narrative. Each milestone symbolizes a step forward and a testament to perseverance and resilience. For someone with Complex PTSD, achieving a goal—no matter how small—can be profoundly affirming. It counters the negative internal dialogue often rooted in traumatic experiences, gradually replacing it with a story of strength and capability.

These celebrations can take various forms, tailored to personal preferences and circumstances. Some may find joy in simply recognizing their progress through reflective journaling, while others might choose to commemorate achievements with supportive friends or family. The key lies in allowing oneself to feel proud of these accomplishments, nurturing a kinder, more compassionate inner voice that acknowledges effort and growth.

This approach effectively strengthens the healing process by reinforcing the belief that change is possible and that personal efforts indeed lead to tangible results. It challenges the often pervasive sense of helplessness associated with trauma, offering a counter-narrative that empowers and inspires continued effort. As individuals celebrate their progress, they rewrite their stories with narratives filled with hope and determination.

Self-Advocacy and Empowerment

Self-advocacy serves as a powerful tool for fostering agency in the recovery process, especially for individuals dealing with Complex PTSD. At its core, self-advocacy involves recognizing one's own needs and learning to articulate them effectively in various seEings, particularly therapeutic ones. This expression does more than simply inform those involved in an individual's care; it fundamentally shifts the dynamic between patient and professional, creating a collaborative approach. By advocating for oneself, an individual acknowledges their intrinsic worth, which is crucial for healing and growth.

In therapeutic environments, voicing one's needs can initially feel daunting. The presence of a therapist or mental health professional may be intimidating to some, due to past experiences or authority dynamics. However, finding the courage to speak up is transformative. It empowers individuals by granting them the opportunity to control their narrative, ensuring that the therapy process is tailored to their unique circumstances. For instance, if a particular therapeutic technique feels overwhelming or ineffective, saying so allows for adjustments that beÉer suit their comfort and progress. This not only enhances the therapeutic relationship but also reinforces the individual's sense of agency.

Effective communication strategies are essential in building confidence when articulating feelings. Clear and assertive communication helps bridge the gap between what one feels internally and how they express it externally. Techniques such as 'I' statements—where one expresses feelings and needs without assigning blame—can facilitate open discussions while minimizing conflict. This approach, "I feel stressed when... I need..." centers the conversation around personal experiences and necessities. Practicing these techniques not only aids in therapy but also transfers to everyday interactions, further boosting one's self-assuredness.

Moreover, advocating for oneself throughout the recovery process significantly supports mental health. When individuals actively participate in shaping their treatment, they often experience lower levels of anxiety and depression. They gain a sense of purpose and direction, as opposed to feeling like passive recipients of care. This active involvement translates into increased motivation and engagement with the healing journey. Self-advocacy thus encourages a proactive stance in mental health management, allowing individuals to recognize and pursue interventions that align with their well-being priorities.

A related and equally important aspect of empowerment lies in exploring self-expression through personal choices. When individuals begin to experiment with decision-making, they realize the breadth of possibilities available to them. Encouraging this exploration strengthens their ability to identify preferences and make informed choices about their lives. Simple daily decisions, like choosing what to wear or eat, can be starting points. Gradually, making larger life decisions becomes less intimidating as confidence grows. This process reflects the broader principle of empowerment: regaining a sense of control over one's path.

To effectively harness the benefits of personal choice exploration, integrating small yet deliberate actions into daily routines can be helpful. For instance, seÈing aside time each day for activities that bring joy or promote relaxation is a practice of self-compassion and autonomy. Whether it's dedicating ten minutes to mindful meditation, taking a leisurely walk, or engaging in a creative hobby, these choices reinforce the belief that one's desires and time are valuable. In doing so, individuals watching their lives transition from surviving to thriving become evident.

Another facet of promoting self-expression through choice is encouraging curiosity. Openness to new experiences broadens understanding and self-awareness. Trying new hobbies, meeting diverse groups of people, or simply visiting unfamiliar places can open doors to previously unconsidered interests and passions. Such endeavors foster resilience, adaptability, and a sense of adventure, cultivating a life that feels vibrant and fulfilling even amid the challenges posed by Complex PTSD.

Additionally, it's important to recognize and celebrate incremental successes in this journey. Acknowledgment of progress, however small, motivates continued efforts. For example, if one successfully communicates a need or makes a decision about their care, pausing to reflect on the achievement bolsters confidence. Similarly, supporting friends and family can play a pivotal role. Their encouragement and recognition of positive changes can fortify the individual's resolve to stay commiÈed to their self-healing path.

Mindfulness and Meditation Techniques

Mindfulness and meditation techniques offer a profound approach to enhancing mental well-being, particularly for those navigating the complexities of Complex PTSD. The practice of mindfulness involves focusing on the present moment, while meditation provides a structured environment to cultivate this awareness. Together, they create a sanctuary where individuals can explore their inner landscapes with compassion and clarity. These practices invite individuals to observe their thoughts and emotions without judgment, thereby fostering a deeper understanding of themselves and their experiences. Encouraging a mindful presence in everyday life, these techniques serve as a gentle invitation to reconnect with the self amidst the chaos and noise that often accompany trauma-induced stress.

Daily Meditation Rituals

Establishing a daily meditation practice can serve as a transformative tool for individuals dealing with Complex PTSD. This subtle yet profound discipline helps cultivate awareness, reduce anxiety, and promote emotional regulation, all of which are crucial in managing PTSD symptoms. Meditation nurtures mindfulness by encouraging individuals to anchor their thoughts and emotions to the present moment. In doing so, it gradually enhances emotional stability, creating a peaceful realm within one's mind where healing can unfold.

Meditation offers a respite from the tumultuous whirlpool of thoughts that often accompany Complex PTSD. By fostering mindfulness, individuals learn to observe their thoughts and feelings without judgment. This non-reactive stance allows for a broader perspective on how these experiences shape behavior and reactions. As practitioners focus on their breath or a particular sensation, they begin to understand the fleeting nature of negative emotions, diminishing their power. The echoes of traumatic memories lose their intensity, replaced by a tranquil, grounded presence.

The benefits of meditation extend beyond mindfulness. It also contributes significantly to mitigating anxiety and restoring emotional equilibrium. For those with Complex PTSD, anxiety can manifest as an overwhelming sense of dread or hyper-vigilance, often triggered by reminders of past trauma. Regular meditation practice can alleviate these symptoms by teaching individuals how to navigate distressing thoughts and emotions without being swept away by them. Over time, the habitual return to a meditative state becomes a sanctuary, a mental safe harbor devoid of anxiety's grip.

Creating a personal routine is pivotal in embedding meditation into daily life. The consistency of practice builds a comforting familiarity, countering the unpredictability that often characterizes PTSD experiences. Choosing a specific time and location for meditation can strengthen commitment and transform it into a cherished ritual. A quiet corner of a room, adorned with calming elements like soft lighting or soothing aromas, can become a dedicated space for reflection. Establishing such a routine need not be restrictive; rather, it serves as an invitation to pause and reconnect with oneself amidst the din of daily responsibilities.

There are innumerable approaches to meditation, allowing each person to tailor their practice according to their needs and preferences. Guided meditations are particularly beneficial for those recovering from trauma, offering structured pathways toward healing. These sessions often incorporate visualization techniques and calming music, specifically curated to address trauma-related challenges. Imagery can act as a bridge, leading the mind away from distress and toward safety and peace. For instance, imagining oneself enveloped in a cocoon of warmth and light can evoke feelings of security, aiding the process of emotional release and recovery.

Guided meditations often focus on fostering resilience and self-compassion. By reimagining traumatic memories through a lens of understanding and acceptance, individuals can rewrite their emotional responses. Calm, soothing music accompanying these sessions further aids relaxation, allowing the nervous system to shift from its fight-or-flight mode to a more restorative state. This synergistic effect deepens the meditative experience, providing a holistic approach to managing PTSD symptoms.

Utilizing technology can enhance access to guided meditations. Various apps and online platforms offer extensive libraries of meditative content tailored specifically for trauma recovery. These resources often feature expert-led sessions designed to resonate with the unique needs of PTSD sufferers. Users can select from a wide range of meditations, focusing on themes like forgiveness, self-love, or leÉing go of past burdens. The flexibility to explore different styles and topics ensures that practitioners find what resonates most profoundly with their personal healing journey.

In addition to guided meditations, some individuals might prefer silent or mantra-based meditation practices. Silence can invite introspection, allowing the innate wisdom of the subconscious to surface. Mantras—simple phrases repeated during meditation—serve as anchors, grounding the mind and preventing it from wandering into distressing territories. Both methods foster a strong internal focus, enhancing the ability to cope with external stimuli and reinforcing emotional resilience.

Creating a Personal Routine

Creating a sustainable meditation schedule is vital for incorporating mindfulness into daily life, especially for individuals diagnosed with Complex PTSD. This thoughtful approach aids in managing symptoms and promotes overall mental health improvement. The first step in establishing such a routine is to start small and build gradually. Beginning with short sessions allows the practice to become part of your daily rhythm without overwhelming you. Five to ten minutes of meditation can be a gentle introduction, easing you into the discipline required for longer periods of focus. As comfort grows and becomes more habitual, you can gradually increase the duration in a manner that feels natural. By doing so, you cultivate patience and self-compassion, acknowledging that progress is personal and unique.

Consistency is another cornerstone when developing a meditation schedule. Allocating a specific time each day for meditation fosters a sense of reliability and commitment. This regularity not only solidifies the practice but also helps anchor it within your daily life. Whether you choose to meditate in the early morning, during a lunch break, or before bedtime, having a consistent time ensures that meditation becomes as integral to your routine as eating meals or brushing your teeth. Equally important is finding a dedicated space for this practice—a quiet corner of a room, a special chair, or even a spot in nature. When you repeatedly return to the same physical space, it increasingly becomes associated with tranquility and focus, helping to strengthen your dedication and progress over time.

Personalizing your meditation practice according to individual preferences is also key to maintaining motivation and adherence. Everyone's experience with meditation can be vastly different, so tailor your practice to fit your needs and comfort level. If you're someone who responds well to music, perhaps playing soft instrumental tunes during meditation will enhance concentration. Alternatively, those who find solace in silence may prefer an environment free from distractions. Exploring different types of meditation—such as guided sessions, breathing exercises, or body scans—allows you to discover what resonates most powerfully with you. Some might find sitting on a cushion beneficial, while others prefer lying down. The goal is to make the practice enjoyable and something to look forward to, rather than a chore.

To sustain long-term practice, consider setting realistic goals that celebrate small victories. Setting intentions like "I will meditate for five days this week" provides structure and purpose, encouraging continued engagement. Recognize that lapses in practice are normal, and rather than viewing them as failures, see them as opportunities to reassess and readjust your approach. You might find using a meditation app or journal useful to track your progress, offering visual encouragement of your journey.

Another effective method to develop a sustainable schedule is seeking community support. Engaging with others who are also practicing meditation can offer encouragement and accountability. Joining a group or class—either virtually or in person—provides a shared experience where insights and challenges can be discussed openly. This communal aspect enriches the practice, providing perspective and camaraderie, crucial elements in sustaining motivation.

In addition, understanding that the benefits of meditation extend beyond immediate relaxation can reinforce its importance in your life. Regular practice has been shown to improve emotional regulation, reduce stress, and enhance mental clarity, particularly important for those managing

Complex PTSD. These benefits, although sometimes gradual, accumulate over time. Reflecting on these changes in mood and mindset serves as a powerful motivator to maintain and even deepen your commitment to meditation.

Finally, integrating mindfulness into various aspects of daily life can fortify the effects of formal meditation practices. Simple acts of mindfulness—such as paying aĖention to your breath during moments of anxiety, savoring a meal without distractions, or noticing the sensations as you walk—can complement your scheduled practice. These brief, informal practices serve as reminders of the calm and awareness cultivated through meditation, making it easier to stay connected to your goals throughout the day.

Guided Meditations

Enhancing your meditation experiences can significantly contribute to managing Complex PTSD symptoms, and utilizing additional resources is a powerful way to do this. With the increasing availability of digital platforms dedicated to mental health and wellness, individuals now have access to a multitude of guided meditation sessions specifically tailored for trauma recovery. These sessions offer structured support that can help users navigate through their healing journey, addressing the unique challenges posed by Complex PTSD.

One of the most effective ways to enhance meditation is by engaging with platforms offering guided sessions. These sessions often incorporate therapeutic techniques designed to address trauma-related issues. For example, apps or websites may provide meditations led by experienced practitioners who understand the nuances of PTSD. This offers a sense of reassurance and trust, enabling individuals to feel safe while exploring their inner worlds. The guidance provided in these sessions can be incredibly beneficial in overcoming feelings of anxiety, fear, and stress associated with past traumatic events.

Platforms like Headspace, Calm, or Insight Timer offer various programs developed specifically for trauma survivors. These programs include beginner-friendly options, as well as more advanced practices, allowing users to progress at their own pace. Importantly, they also frequently offer community forums where participants can share experiences and lend mutual support, creating an environment of shared understanding and empathy.

In addition to professional guidance, incorporating elements such as guided imagery and calming sounds into your practice can deepen relaxation and focus. Guided imagery involves visualizing peaceful and safe seÈings, helping to shift aÈention away from distressing thoughts. This technique can be particularly valuable for those with Complex PTSD, as it provides a controlled space where the mind can retreat and recharge.

Calming sounds, such as gentle music, nature sounds, or ambient noise, can further enhance the meditative experience. These sounds work as auditory anchors, maintaining focus and grounding the listener in the present moment. Often, these elements are intentionally chosen to lower stress levels and induce a state of calmness. By combining guided imagery with calming sounds, practitioners can create a sanctuary for themselves, a mental retreat that offers a reprieve from the intensity of everyday life.

Practicing guided meditations that have been specifically designed for Complex PTSD can make a significant difference in managing its symptoms. Unlike generalized meditation practices, these sessions take into account the specific needs and sensitivities of individuals with past trauma. They often incorporate mindfulness practices aimed at reducing hypervigilance, soothing heightened emotional responses, and promoting self-compassion.

Moreover, these specialized meditations use language and exercises that acknowledge the lived experiences of trauma survivors. This acknowledgment is crucial in fostering a sense of validation and recognizing the complexity of the healing process. Techniques such as body scanning, progressive muscle relaxation, and grounding exercises are commonly used in these sessions to regulate emotional states and encourage a connection between mind and body.

For instance, a body scan can help increase awareness of physical sensations, allowing individuals to discern areas of tension or discomfort and subsequently release them. Meanwhile, grounding exercises encourage a focus on the immediate physical environment, drawing aÉention away from intrusive thoughts or flashbacks—a frequent challenge for those with Complex PTSD.

It's worth noting that while engaging with these resources, consistency is key. Regular practice strengthens the benefits gained from meditation, potentially leading to greater emotional stability and improved mental health over time. Therefore, integrating a routine that includes guided meditation can serve as an anchor, providing stability amidst the unpredictability of daily life.

By leveraging these additional resources, individuals can enrich their meditation journeys, achieving deeper levels of relaxation and understanding. As these practices become integral to one's routine, the impact on mental health can be profound, offering a pathway not only to manage symptoms but to foster long-term resilience and healing.

Ultimately, these varied approaches underscore the importance of having supportive tools and structures in place when dealing with Complex PTSD. Whether through digital platforms, guided imagery, or specialized meditations, the goal remains the same: to empower individuals in reclaiming their peace and cultivating a sense of safety within themselves. Through mindful engagement with these resources, one can steadily navigate the complexities of trauma and embrace a journey toward healing with hope and compassion.

Mindfulness Exercises Integrated into Daily Life

Integrating mindfulness into everyday activities can serve as a powerful tool to enhance emotional awareness, particularly for individuals managing Complex PTSD. By embedding mindfulness into daily routines, one can cultivate a more profound connection with their thoughts and emotions, which can significantly aid in trauma recovery.

One effective way to incorporate mindfulness into daily life is through mindful breathing techniques. These techniques provide a simple yet potent means of recentering thoughts and reducing stress when one's mind becomes overwhelmed or triggered. Breathing exercises encourage focusing solely on the breath, helping to anchor the mind and steer it away from distressing thoughts. For example, taking slow, deliberate breaths while counting each inhale and exhale can create a sense of calm and control, especially during moments of heightened anxiety. This practice not only soothes the nervous system but also increases one's awareness of how their body responds to stress. Over time, this increased awareness can help individuals identify and manage their emotional triggers more effectively.

Another practice that serves to enhance emotional awareness is the body scan technique. This method involves paying close aĖention to various parts of the body, one at a time, to notice any tension or discomfort and acknowledge feelings that arise without judgment. As individuals mentally "scan" their bodies, they become more aĖuned to physical sensations and how these relate to emotional states. For someone dealing with Complex PTSD, recognizing these connections can be pivotal in releasing stored emotional stress. The body scan can act as a gentle reminder that emotions and physical sensations are interconnected, encouraging a holistic approach to healing. Practicing this technique regularly can contribute to a greater understanding of one's emotional responses, thereby aiding in self-regulation and recovery.

Incorporating mindfulness into routine tasks, such as walking or washing dishes, offers another avenue for cultivating presence and appreciation in everyday life. Often, mundane activities are performed on autopilot, allowing the mind to wander or ruminate on stressors. By engaging in these tasks mindfully, individuals can transform them into opportunities for grounding and focus. While walking, one might pay attention to the sensation of the ground beneath their feet, the rhythm of their steps, or the surrounding environment. Similarly, while washing dishes, the warmth of the water, the texture of the soap, and the movement of the hands can all serve as focal points for mindfulness. These seemingly simple acts encourage living in the moment, fostering a deeper appreciation for life's small details and helping to shift the mind away from distressing thoughts.

To enhance the integration of mindfulness practices into daily life and monitor progress, keeping a meditation journal can be incredibly beneficial. Tracking moods, emotional shifts, and insights gained from mindfulness exercises allows individuals to reflect on their journey and pinpoint which techniques resonate most with them. This structured reflection not only helps in recognizing patterns but also provides motivation by highlighting improvements over time. Furthermore, sharing journaling experiences with others in support groups or mindfulness communities can offer encouragement and facilitate deeper understanding. Engaging with peers who share similar challenges can create a network of support, enhancing both personal growth and social connection.

Reflecting on progress through written documentation, such as a meditation journal, can maintain momentum and illuminate the benefits of consistent practice. Reflection serves as a powerful tool for recognizing growth and understanding how different mindfulness methods impact one's mental health. By documenting successes and setbacks alike, individuals gain valuable insights into their own behaviors and coping mechanisms, enabling them to make informed adjustments to their mindfulness routines. This ongoing self-awareness strengthens resilience, fosters self-compassion, and underscores the healing potential of incorporating mindfulness into everyday life.

Moreover, connecting with a meditation community offers opportunities to share experiences, learn from others, and receive constructive feedback. Communities provide a safe space for discussing mindfulness practices, exchanging tips, and gaining new perspectives. Participating in group discussions or aĖending mindfulness workshops can deepen one's practice and reinforce commitment to personal well-being. Additionally, hearing about others' journeys and triumphs can inspire hope and remind individuals that they are not alone in their struggles. Building these connections fosters a sense of belonging and validates the shared endeavor of navigating Complex PTSD together.

Tracking Progress

Monitoring changes in mental health can be a transformative tool for individuals with Complex PTSD, as it allows them to observe how mindfulness practices like meditation influence their journey toward healing. The process facilitates deeper understanding and acknowledgment of emotional shifts and growth over time. One effective method for monitoring these changes is by keeping a meditation journal. This simple yet powerful practice encourages individuals to record their thoughts, feelings, and experiences before and after meditation sessions.

A meditation journal serves as a personal reflection space where one can write about what they felt during their practice and any emotions that surfaced afterward. It offers an opportunity to recognize paĖerns in thoughts and behaviors. For those dealing with Complex PTSD, recording these observations can highlight subtle changes in emotional responses, resilience, and self-awareness. Over weeks and months, this recorded history becomes a narrative of growth and adaptation, revealing the incremental progress often overlooked in day-to-day life.

For example, a person might notice through journaling that certain triggers have become less intense over time, or that periods of calm and clarity are lasting longer after meditation. These insights can be encouraging and serve as tangible evidence that mindfulness practices are making a difference. Moreover, this reflective process can help individuals set intentions for future meditation sessions, focusing on areas they wish to explore or improve, thus making each session more purposeful and directed.

Reflecting on progress through structured reflection not only highlights personal growth but also provides motivation to continue practicing. Motivation can fluctuate, especially when dealing with the complexities of PTSD, but seeing documented evidence of change can rekindle the dedication needed to maintain regular practice. This ongoing reflection creates a positive feedback loop; the more progress is acknowledged, the more one is inclined to engage in mindfulness practices, anticipating further development.

To strengthen this commitment, individuals might set small, attainable goals within their journaling practice. For instance, aiming to meditate for a specific number of days consecutively or exploring different techniques and documenting their effects could be motivating. Achieving these small milestones boosts confidence and reinforces personal belief in the effectiveness of their practice. It demonstrates a clear connection between effort and outcome, which is particularly empowering for someone managing Complex PTSD symptoms.

Beyond individual reflection, sharing experiences within a community can offer additional layers of encouragement and insight. Participating in groups—whether in-person meet-ups or online forums—can enable individuals to exchange stories, challenges, and successes related to their meditation journeys. Such interactions can be incredibly affirming; realizing that others are on similar paths fosters a sense of belonging and reduces the isolation often experienced by those dealing with trauma-related conditions.

Community engagement also opens up opportunities to learn from others' experiences. Listening to different approaches and coping strategies enhances understanding and may inspire new ways to integrate mindfulness into one's life. For example, someone might learn about a breathing technique or visual imagery exercise they hadn't considered before, which might resonate profoundly with them. Additionally, being part of a group dedicated to similar goals can create a supportive environment where encouragement is readily available, forming a safety net that cushions members during difficult times.

While personal progress is crucial, the shared stories within a community can offer validation and reassurance that others have walked similar paths and found solace. Understanding that recovery is not linear, and witnessing others' ups and downs can provide a broader perspective on one's own journey. It emphasizes the importance of patience and persistence and validates the various emotions experienced along the way.

Conversations in these communities can also highlight the diverse benefits of mindfulness beyond what one might initially expect. Members might discuss improvements in focus, enhanced creativity, or better sleep quality—all potentially significant for someone managing the cognitive and emotional difficulties associated with Complex PTSD. Hearing about these unexpected gains can reinforce the practice's value and encourage a more comprehensive view of its benefits.

In cultivating both individual and communal reflection, it's essential to approach the practice of journaling and sharing with kindness and non-judgment. Emotions and progress may vary widely, and accepting this variability without self-criticism is vital. Encouraging a non-linear understanding of healing allows individuals to embrace each step forward as meaningful, even if setbacks occur. This mindset sustains a compassionate approach to personal and collective healing.

Therapy Techniques for Complex PTSD

Managing Complex PTSD involves understanding the intricacies of therapy techniques that are specifically designed to address its unique challenges. This chapter delves into various therapeutic approaches aimed at helping individuals navigate the symptoms and emotional complexities associated with Complex PTSD. The journey of healing from such deep-seated trauma requires more than traditional methods, urging a need for specialized strategies. Therapy becomes a space of hope and resilience, where individuals learn not only to cope but thrive beyond their past traumas. This complex landscape wherein trauma intersects with recovery is explored in depth, offering an empathetic yet insightful examination of what it truly means to move toward healing.

Cognitive-behavioral Techniques

Cognitive-behavioral strategies are essential tools in managing Complex PTSD. One of the foundational components of this approach involves identifying distorted thoughts that contribute to emotional distress. Distorted thoughts often manifest as automatic negative beliefs about oneself or the world, such as "I am unworthy" or "The world is a dangerous place." These thoughts perpetuate feelings of anxiety and depression, acting as barriers to healing. To tackle this, individuals must first become aware of these distortions through self-monitoring, journaling, or guided therapy sessions. Once identified, it becomes possible to challenge these thought paÉerns by questioning their validity, considering alternative viewpoints, and replacing them with more balanced thoughts. For instance, if someone believes they are unlovable due to past trauma, supportive evidence and feedback from trusted peers can help reframe this belief into one that is more compassionate and truthful.

In addition to addressing distorted thoughts, engaging in activities that promote emotional well-being and reduce avoidance behaviors is crucial for recovery. People with Complex PTSD may find themselves avoiding situations, people, or places that remind them of past traumas, causing their world to become increasingly smaller and less fulfilling. Gradual exposure to these avoided experiences, facilitated in a supportive environment, helps individuals regain control over their lives. This process, known as behavioral activation, encourages individuals to partake in meaningful activities that once brought joy and satisfaction. Through gradual re-engagement, whether it's hobbies, social events, or simple daily routines, individuals can slowly start to rebuild their sense of autonomy and enjoyment, thereby diminishing the power trauma holds over them.

Techniques for disputing irrational beliefs and reframing dysfunctional beliefs further aid in fostering a more balanced perspective. Irrational beliefs are rigid, extreme, and often inaccurate perceptions that skew an individual's understanding of themselves and their circumstances. They tend to surface as all-or-nothing thinking, catastrophizing, or blaming. By employing cognitive restructuring, individuals learn to identify these beliefs, understand their origins, and systematically dispute them. This involves asking critical questions like "What is the evidence for and against this belief?" or "How might someone else interpret this situation?" Over time, practicing these techniques supports the development of flexible thinking paEerns that promote resilience. By reshaping their cognition, individuals begin to view challenges not as insurmountable obstacles but as opportunities for growth and adaptation, which is vital for long-term healing.

Mindfulness practices provide additional support within cognitive-behavioral frameworks by enhancing self-awareness and emotional regulation. Mindfulness involves paying aEention to the present moment without judgment, allowing individuals to observe their thoughts and emotions as they arise. This non-reactive awareness creates a space where individuals can choose how to respond to their internal experiences, rather than being driven by them. In practice, mindfulness can be integrated into daily life through simple exercises such as mindful breathing, body scans, or meditation. It bolsters emotional regulation by helping individuals recognize triggers and manage stress responses effectively. For those dealing with Complex PTSD, cultivating mindfulness offers a pathway to greater emotional stability and increased insight into their mental processes, contributing to a more profound sense of peace and control over their recovery journey.

Each of these cognitive-behavioral strategies requires commitment and patience, as they do not offer instant results but lead to substantial benefits over time. The journey involves both challenges and triumphs, demanding perseverance and continuous effort. Individuals are encouraged to collaborate closely with mental health professionals who can guide them through these strategies, tailoring interventions to suit their unique needs and circumstances. Family members and loved ones can also play a supportive role by understanding these approaches, offering empathy, and encouraging progress without pressure.

Introduction to EMDR Therapy

Eye Movement Desensitization and Reprocessing (EMDR) is an innovative therapeutic approach that has gained recognition for its effectiveness in treating Complex PTSD. Unlike traditional talk therapy, EMDR targets the root of trauma by facilitating the brain's natural healing processes. At the core of EMDR is the belief that traumatic memories can be stored incorrectly in the brain, causing distress long after the event has passed. EMDR helps reprocess these memories, reducing their emotional charge and enabling individuals to heal from past traumas.

The mechanism behind EMDR involves a combination of cognitive and sensory processing. During an EMDR session, a therapist guides the client through recalling traumatic experiences while simultaneously engaging in bilateral stimulation—this can include eye movements, taps, or sounds. This dual aĖention stimulus is believed to help the brain reprocess disturbing memories more adaptively. By doing so, individuals may find relief from persistent symptoms like nightmares, flashbacks, and intense emotional reactions, which are common in Complex PTSD.

A structured roadmap for EMDR therapy consists of eight distinct phases. These phases provide a comprehensive framework to ensure effective treatment and foster healing. The first phase involves history taking and treatment planning, where the therapist gathers information about the client's history and identifies target memories for reprocessing. Next is preparation, where the client learns coping strategies for dealing with emotional distress. The third phase, assessment, involves identifying specific negative beliefs associated with traumatic memories and establishing positive beliefs the client would prefer to have.

The fourth phase, desensitization, is where bilateral stimulation occurs while the client focuses on traumatic memory and associated distress. This process continues until the distress diminishes significantly. Installation, the fifth phase, focuses on strengthening a positive belief about themselves, which replaces the negative belief connected to the trauma. During the sixth phase, body scan, clients identify any residual physical tension linked to the memory, addressing it to reduce physical symptoms of distress.

Closure, the seventh phase, brings each session to a safe conclusion, ensuring the client leaves feeling stable. Finally, reevaluation, the eighth phase, monitors the progress and determines if further sessions are needed. Together, these phases form a thorough blueprint for navigating EMDR therapy, ensuring each step is tailored to aid recovery.

Support for EMDR's potential comes from numerous case studies and success stories that underscore its transformative impact. For instance, take Sarah, who endured early childhood trauma leading to severe anxiety and depression. After several EMDR sessions, Sarah reported significant reductions in her symptoms. The troubling images and emotions she once experienced daily became distant and less intrusive. Her journey reflects countless similar experiences, showing that EMDR can profoundly change how individuals live with Complex PTSD.

Several studies have demonstrated EMDR's efficacy, bringing scientific validation to personal testimonies. Research has shown that EMDR is not only effective but often works more quickly than other therapeutic approaches, offering hope for those eager to see tangible improvements in their mental health.

Choosing a qualified EMDR therapist is crucial for successful treatment. A good starting point is finding therapists certified by recognized bodies, such as the EMDR International Association. Certification ensures the therapist has undergone specialized training and adheres to professional standards. It's important to feel comfortable with your therapist, as trust and rapport significantly influence therapy outcomes.

When evaluating potential therapists, consider asking about their experience with EMDR and working with clients who have Complex PTSD. Inquire about the number of sessions typically recommended and what you can expect during treatment. Transparency and openness about the process will help set realistic expectations and create a pathway toward recovery.

Finding an EMDR therapist might also involve considering logistical factors such as location, availability, and cost. Therapy requires commitment, and these practical concerns can affect one's ability to remain engaged in the treatment process over time. Additionally, some insurance plans may cover EMDR sessions, so it's worth investigating this possibility to make therapy more accessible.

In summary, EMDR offers a promising avenue for those baEling Complex PTSD, providing a structured yet flexible approach to healing. Its focus on reprocessing traumatic memories allows for profound emotional relief, and many clients report a lighter psychological burden after completing the therapy. Through evidence-based practices and numerous success stories, EMDR stands out as a beacon of hope for lasting recovery.

Behavioral Activation Strategies

Engaging in activities that combat avoidance and foster emotional well-being is a crucial aspect of managing Complex PTSD. This engagement is often challenging, as individuals with Complex PTSD may find themselves stuck in cycles of avoidance due to past trauma. However, re-engaging with enjoyable activities can gradually restore a sense of joy and normalcy.

Understanding the significance of this gradual reconnection is the first step towards healing.

Many individuals with Complex PTSD tend to withdraw from previously enjoyed activities as a protective measure against potential distress or reminders of trauma. Such avoidance might feel safe initially but can inadvertently lead to isolation and depression. It is vital to recognize that re-engagement should be a gentle process. Starting with small, manageable steps can make a significant difference. For instance, if gardening once brought joy, spending just ten minutes a day tending to plants can be an excellent starting point. Over time, these brief moments can evolve into longer, more fulfilling sessions, creating a positive feedback loop of enjoyment and accomplishment.

To aid this gradual re-engagement, developing specific strategies to integrate small behavioral changes into daily routines can be highly beneficial. These strategies need not be complex; rather, they should be practical and realistic, catering to individual preferences and lifestyle. One effective approach is seEing a daily routine that includes at least one activity geared toward personal enjoyment or relaxation. For example, incorporating a short walk into a daily schedule can serve both as physical exercise and an opportunity for mental rejuvenation. The key is consistency—committing to even a few minutes a day can foster a habit of engagement, leading to longer participation times as comfort levels increase.

In line with this strategy, it's also important to encourage the celebration of small victories. Recognizing and appreciating these achievements can significantly boost self-efficacy and motivation, critical components in the healing journey. Achievements could be as simple as completing a short workout, cooking a homemade meal, or finishing a chapter of a book. Marking these successes helps reinforce the notion that progress is being made, building confidence over time. Keeping a journal to track such accomplishments can provide visual evidence of growth and resilience, serving as a motivational tool on tougher days.

Highlighting activities that align with personal values is another powerful way to maintain consistency and interest. Activities deeply rooted in personal beliefs or passions are more likely to sustain one's aĖention and commitment. For someone who values creativity, engaging in arts and crafts, writing, or playing a musical instrument can be immensely rewarding. Similarly, those who value helping others might find fulfillment in volunteering. Aligning activities with core values ensures that they are not merely duties but rather fulfilling experiences that enrich life.

It's equally important to involve supportive friends and family members in this process, when possible, to foster a sense of community and connection. Loved ones can play an integral role by offering encouragement and participating in activities together. Their support can make transitions smoother and more enjoyable, providing additional motivation and accountability.

However, re-engagement should always respect personal limits and pace. Emotional and physical boundaries must be honored to prevent overwhelming feelings or setbacks. It's perfectly acceptable to pause or take breaks when needed. Recovery is not a sprint but a marathon, requiring patience and self-compassion. Progress might come in waves, with periods of advancement followed by plateaus or slight regressions. Acknowledging this natural ebb and flow can alleviate undue pressure and stress while maintaining focus on long-term goals.

Cognitive Restructuring Techniques

In the journey of managing Complex PTSD, individuals often encounter deeply entrenched irrational beliefs that can act as barriers to recovery. Identifying and challenging these cognitive distortions is crucial in paving the way toward healing. Many people carry beliefs such as "I am unlovable" or "The world is unsafe," which can exacerbate symptoms by reinforcing a negative self-view and perception of the environment.

A practical approach to identifying these beliefs is through thought monitoring. This involves actively observing and recording thoughts as they arise throughout the day. By doing so, individuals can begin to recognize patterns and triggers associated with negative beliefs. Thought records, which track situations, emotions, and reactions, can be particularly effective tools. Once identified, the next step is disputing these irrational beliefs. By questioning their validity, individuals learn to differentiate between evidence-based facts and distorted perceptions. Techniques like Socratic questioning—where one asks themselves probing questions about the belief—can help unravel these misconceptions.

Reframing negative thoughts positively is another important aspect of challenging dysfunctional beliefs. This doesn't mean ignoring reality but rather choosing to view experiences through a more balanced lens. For instance, someone may feel they failed an obligation, leading to the belief, "I always mess things up." Reframing could involve recognizing mistakes as opportunities for growth and emphasizing what was learned rather than what went wrong. Cognitive restructuring exercises focus on substituting negative thoughts with constructive alternatives. Over time, this practice encourages a more optimistic outlook, which is essential for overcoming Complex PTSD.

Furthermore, reframing thinking patterns is not only about changing perspectives but also about cultivating increased self-acceptance and compassion—the cornerstones of mental health resilience. Often, those struggling with Complex PTSD harbor feelings of guilt and shame stemming from past trauma. Restructuring cognition can alleviate these burdens by fostering a kind and accepting attitude towards oneself. Self-compassion exercises, such as writing a letter to yourself expressing kindness and understanding, can reinforce these positive changes. Emphasizing progress over perfection helps nurture a sense of self-worth and acceptance, crucial for sustaining long-term recovery.

Another key to managing symptoms lies in building resilience and flexibility in thinking. Inflexible thought paĖerns undermine emotional health, keeping individuals trapped in cycles of negativity. Developing resilience involves practicing adaptability in one's interpretations and responses to challenges. Cognitive-behavioral techniques teach how to pivot thoughts and adaptively respond to unexpected situations, enhancing one's capacity to cope with stressors effectively.

One method for cultivating resilience is engaging in mindfulness-based cognitive therapy (MBCT), which integrates mindfulness practices to heighten awareness of the present moment. Mindfulness encourages non-judgmental observation of thoughts and emotions, helping individuals step back from rumination and worry. Through consistent practice, mindfulness nurtures a flexible mindset and opens up new pathways for healthier emotional regulation. Incorporating meditation or breathing exercises into daily routines can support this process, promoting tranquility and clarity in thought.

Additionally, therapeutic strategies like acceptance and commitment therapy (ACT) can bolster cognitive flexibility. ACT encourages the acceptance of difficult emotions and thoughts rather than engaging in struggles to change them. This acceptance allows individuals to shift focus from trying to control internal experiences to taking meaningful action aligned with personal values. ACT techniques verify the notion that even amidst adversity, one can choose actions that reflect deeper aspirations and goals, enhancing emotional well-being and life satisfaction.

Mindfulness Integration in Therapy

Mindfulness, a practice rooted in ancient traditions and embraced by modern psychology, offers significant benefits for individuals managing Complex PTSD. Through its integration into therapeutic processes, mindfulness can enhance the effectiveness of cognitive strategies used in treatment. By focusing on the present moment without judgment, mindfulness allows individuals to develop an awareness that can be transformative.

One practical approach to incorporating mindfulness is through exercises such as mindful breathing or body scanning. These exercises encourage individuals to pay close aĖention to their breathing paĖerns or the sensations within their bodies. Such practices help to disconnect from intrusive memories or overwhelming emotions often experienced in Complex PTSD, offering a reprieve and promoting emotional regulation. For example, starting a session with deep breathing can center the mind, easing tension and preparing it for processing therapeutic content more effectively.

Developing mindfulness practices serves as a vital grounding tool during moments of distress. People with Complex PTSD may experience flashbacks or bouts of anxiety triggered by reminders of past traumas. Mindfulness exercises like grounding techniques—where one focuses intently on the physical environment using the five senses—can redirect aĖention away from distressing thoughts. This method not only alleviates immediate stress but also helps build resilience over time, providing strength and stability when faced with triggers.

Furthermore, mindfulness creates space for intentional thought paĖerns and reactions. In the midst of psychological turmoil, automatic responses often arise, driven by ingrained paĖerns formed during traumatic experiences. Mindfulness encourages a pause—a space where individuals can observe these reactions, identify them without judgment, and then choose more intentional, adaptive responses. It nurtures the ability to respond rather than react, fostering healthier communication and interaction paĖerns in everyday life.

By practicing mindfulness consistently, individuals can cultivate self-awareness and acceptance, key components for mental stability. Self-awareness derived from mindfulness involves recognizing one's emotions, thoughts, and physiological responses as they arise. It provides insight into how these elements interconnect and affect one's wellbeing. Acceptance, another pillar supported by mindfulness, involves embracing one's experiences without resistance. For those with Complex PTSD, accepting experiences as part of their narrative, without being overwhelmed by them, contributes to healing.

Promoting self-awareness through mindfulness also leads to greater understanding of personal triggers and stressors. By closely observing their own responses, individuals gain insights into what affects them and how. This self-knowledge empowers them to engage proactively in therapy, working collaboratively with therapists to tailor interventions that address their specific needs.

The practice of mindfulness doesn't stop at creating internal harmony; it extends to interpersonal relationships as well. Enhanced self-awareness fosters empathy and understanding, crucial elements in rebuilding connections with others that may have been strained due to past trauma-related behaviors. Being present in interactions, free from the burden of past regrets or future anxieties, enriches relationships and supports the development of a supportive community around the individual.

Importantly, integrating mindfulness into therapeutic practices doesn't require drastic life changes or extended time commitments. Simple daily mindfulness practices, integrated into routine activities like eating, walking, or even brushing teeth, can make a substantial difference. By teaching individuals to apply mindfulness in manageable increments, therapists can empower clients to maintain consistency and reap long-term benefits.

Finally, mindfulness establishes a foundation for ongoing personal growth beyond therapy sessions. By instilling a mindset of curiosity and openness, it encourages continual self-exploration and development. Even as symptoms of Complex PTSD are managed, mindfulness supports lifelong resiliency, helping individuals adapt to new challenges while maintaining inner peace and balance.

Physical Health and PTSD

Exploring the intricate link between physical health and Complex PTSD recovery reveals how interconnected our bodies and minds truly are. The journey of healing from trauma is not only about addressing emotional scars but also about nurturing the body, which acts as both a refuge and a tool for empowerment. Understanding this connection is vital for those who may feel trapped by past experiences yet yearn for a path forward. When we tap into the potential of our physical selves, we open doors to resilience and strength that might have seemed inaccessible before. This chapter aims to shed light on how exercise and nutrition become more than just physical activities—they transform into vessels of healing, fostering a profound sense of well-being.

Exercise as a Tool for Stress Management

Exercise serves as a natural remedy for alleviating the symptoms of Complex PTSD. By engaging in regular physical activity, individuals can harness the powerful benefits of endorphins, which act as nature's own stress relievers. These chemical compounds, released during exercise, help reduce stress levels and provide immediate relief from anxiety. The invigorating feeling post-exercise often results in a mood boost, creating a sense of calm that can be both rejuvenating and liberating.

Beyond the biochemical, physical activity promotes a stronger, healthier body, paving the way to build resilience. When you cultivate physical strength, it often translates into psychological empowerment. This connection can significantly enhance self-esteem, helping individuals with Complex PTSD feel more competent and capable. Engaging in structured routines like running, swimming, or even walking helps reinforce this empowerment. With each completed workout, there's a growing realization of one's potential, offering hope and motivation to continue moving forward.

Moreover, group exercises introduce a social component that is crucial in reducing feelings of isolation—a common experience among those dealing with PTSD. Participating in team sports, joining fitness classes, or even partaking in community events not only provides physical benefits but also creates an opportunity for social interaction. These shared experiences allow individuals to form connections, fostering a supportive environment that encourages openness and understanding, thus mitigating loneliness.

Activities such as yoga and tai chi offer unique opportunities to explore the mind-body connection. These practices emphasize bodily awareness and mindfulness, key aspects in trauma processing. Through deliberate movements and controlled breathing, participants are guided towards a heightened state of alertness and presence. This can be incredibly grounding, helping individuals process traumatic experiences while integrating a sense of control over their bodies and minds. The meditative elements of these activities also nurture inner peace, contributing positively to emotional regulation.

It's important to highlight how diverse forms of exercise cater to different preferences, ensuring there's something for everyone. Whether it's high-intensity workouts for those who thrive on adrenaline or calmer, introspective practices like yoga for those seeking tranquility, the goal is to find an activity that resonates personally and fits seamlessly into one's lifestyle. Incorporating physical activity doesn't require drastic measures; it could be as simple as taking daily walks or stretching regularly—actions that cumulatively make a significant impact.

For those starting out, setting realistic, achievable goals is vital to avoid overwhelm. Consider beginning with a few minutes of light activity a day, gradually increasing duration and intensity as comfort levels rise. This steady progression helps reinforce positive habits while preventing burnout. Within this context, consulting with healthcare providers can provide additional guidance, helping to tailor activity plans that align with specific needs and conditions, ensuring safety and maximizing benefits.

In addition, technology can play a supportive role in maintaining consistency. Fitness apps and online communities offer resources, allowing individuals to track progress, set reminders, and even connect with others pursuing similar goals. These digital tools can serve as motivational aids, providing insight into personal achievements and encouraging accountability.

The journey towards integrating regular exercise into daily routines is deeply personal and requires patience. It's about discovering what feels best and sustaining it over time. Celebrating small victories along the way reinforces the positive association with physical activity, making it a source of joy rather than obligation.

Encouragingly, numerous studies have shown that consistent exercise decreases anxiety episodes and improves overall mood. Over time, these effects contribute to a more stable emotional state, enhancing quality of life. In turn, the rhythmic nature of many exercises introduces a meditative state that promotes mental clarity, helping individuals manage intrusive thoughts or flashbacks associated with PTSD.

Nutritional Basics for Mental Health

Nutrition plays a pivotal role in shaping our mental health and managing symptoms associated with Complex PTSD. A deeper understanding of the nutrients that influence brain function can be immensely beneficial, particularly when it comes to Omega-3 fatty acids and B vitamins. These nutrients are crucial for maintaining optimal brain health. Deficiencies in these vital components can exacerbate symptoms of depression and anxiety, which are often prevalent in individuals grappling with Complex PTSD.

Omega-3s are found abundantly in fish like salmon, mackerel, and sardines, and they are known for their anti-inflammatory properties that support healthy brain function. Incorporating these foods into one's diet can help combat inflammation that may contribute to emotional distress. Similarly, B vitamins, including B6, B12, and folate, play an important role in producing neurotransmitters, such as serotonin and dopamine, which regulate mood. By ensuring adequate intake of these vitamins through sources like whole grains, eggs, and leafy greens, individuals can potentially alleviate some symptoms linked to mood disturbances.

Moving beyond individual nutrients, the concept of a balanced diet emerges as a cornerstone for maintaining brain health. A well-rounded diet not only assists in physical well-being but also significantly impacts mental stability. By stabilizing blood sugar levels, a balanced diet helps reduce the likelihood of sudden mood swings. Consuming regular meals that combine carbohydrates with proteins and fats can prevent the dips and spikes in energy and mood that can occur throughout the day. Foods like nuts, seeds, fruits, vegetables, lean meats, and whole grains form part of a balanced diet that supports sustained energy levels and emotional equilibrium.

In addition to supporting steady energy and mood, certain foods contain properties that directly combat inflammation—a key factor in both physical and mental health issues. Anti-inflammatory foods, rich in antioxidants and Omega-3s, act as allies in the quest for mental clarity and emotional balance. Berries, for example, are packed with antioxidants that fight oxidative stress within the brain, while walnuts and flaxseeds offer plant-based sources of Omega-3s. Integrating these foods into daily meals can create a nourishing foundation for those seeking relief from the overwhelm of stress and anxiety commonly experienced in PTSD.

Conversely, the impact of processed foods on mental well-being cannot be overlooked. Processed foods, which are typically high in sugar, unhealthy fats, and additives, have been linked to adverse effects on emotional health.

Such diets can lead to increased inflammation and disrupt the delicate balance of gut bacteria, which has a direct connection to brain health. The consumption of fast food, sugary drinks, and pre-packaged snacks might provide temporary gratification but often at the expense of long-term mental stability. Studies suggest that diets high in processed foods correlate with an elevated risk of depression.

Making mindful choices around food, therefore, becomes not just a maÈer of physical health, but a strategy for ushering in mental peace and resilience. Establishing routines that prioritize whole, nutrient-dense foods over convenient but less nutritious options requires effort and commitment. However, the rewards—reduced symptoms of anxiety and depression, enhanced mood stability, and an overall sense of well-being—can serve as powerful motivators for change.

For individuals diagnosed with Complex PTSD, as well as their supportive networks, understanding nutrition's impact offers a pathway toward empowerment and healing. In practical terms, this means engaging with the transformative potential of what we eat every day. It involves recognizing the correlation between individual food choices and the broader goal of symptom management. Small changes, like choosing oatmeal over a sugary breakfast cereal, or opting for water instead of soda, accumulate over time, leading to profound shifts in how one feels and functions.

Hydration and Cognitive Function

In the recovery process from Complex PTSD, understanding the physiological needs of the body can often be overlooked, yet they are crucial for mental clarity and overall well-being. One such need is hydration. Remaining well-hydrated is vital for ensuring sustained cognitive function, which is paramount for those managing the challenges of PTSD.

Dehydration poses a serious threat due to its subtle but significant impacts on mental health. A lack of adequate water intake can lead to fatigue. This isn't simply a maÈer of feeling tired; it influences how we interact with our environment and perform daily tasks. Fatigue isn't just physical; it permeates into one's ability to concentrate and process emotions effectively. Mood swings, another consequence of dehydration, can become more pronounced, making emotional management a tougher baÈle. Cognitive impairment stands as one of the most severe outcomes, affecting memory, aÈention, and decision-making abilities. Each of these factors heavily influences daily activities and the broader journey towards healing from PTSD.

Moreover, staying hydrated has direct implications for mental focus. Adequate water consumption acts as a tool to enhance one's focus and overall mental clarity. Imagine trying to read a book with foggy glasses; no maÈer how hard you try, understanding the content becomes almost impossible. In a similar vein, dehydration clouds our capacity to think clearly, making the path to recovery seem more turbulent. Hydration, therefore, becomes a simple yet effective measure in promoting smoother cognitive processes. As the mind clears, the recovery experience transforms from an uphill struggle to a more manageable journey. This paradigm shift reinforces a positive feedback loop, where improved cognition fuels further engagement in recovery activities, ultimately accelerating the healing process.

As individuals venture into physical activities to aid their recovery efforts, the role of hydration takes on heightened significance. Physical exertion naturally leads to fluid loss through sweat, necessitating a proactive approach to replenish these vital fluids. Engaging in exercise provides numerous benefits for both physical and mental health, yet without proper hydration, these advantages can be diminished. The brain relies on well-functioning neurological pathways, especially during physical activities that challenge coordination and motor skills. Dehydration hampers these pathways, leading to delayed reactions and reduced cognitive performance when it's needed most. Thus, maintaining hydration before, during, and after any form of physical activity not only supports physical endurance but also ensures that cognitive performance remains optimized. This allows individuals to fully reap the benefits of their physical endeavors, fostering greater resilience over time.

Implementing straightforward strategies to maintain optimal hydration levels throughout the day can significantly ease this process. Carrying a water boÉle serves as a constant reminder to drink regularly and is a tangible way to track water intake. Setting periodic reminders on digital devices or incorporating hydration into daily routines, like drinking a glass of water with each meal, can develop consistent habits. Some might find infusing water with slices of fruit or herbs makes drinking water more enjoyable. Additionally, it's important to recognize how external factors, such as climate and activity level, can influence individual hydration needs. During hoÉer months or days filled with intense activities, increasing water intake is necessary to balance additional moisture loss.

For those who find themselves struggling with remembering to hydrate, gradual changes may prove beneficial. Starting with small, achievable goals like drinking a glass of water in the morning upon waking can pave the way toward habitual practices. Viewing hydration as an integral part of self-care, rather than an obligation, transforms it into a personal commitment to wellness, echoing the larger narrative of recovery from PTSD. These simple adjustments not only enhance physical health but also empower individuals, providing them with a sense of control and autonomy in their recovery journey.

Hydration may appear as a basic necessity at first glance, yet its importance extends deeply into our mental faculties and emotional stability—it upholds the very foundation of cognitive function essential for navigating the complexities of PTSD recovery. By prioritizing hydration, individuals equip themselves with a potent tool to counteract the detrimental effects of dehydration, thereby elevating their capacity to engage in various therapeutic activities. The benefits extend beyond mental clarity, influencing mood regulation and facilitating emotional resilience. This underscores hydration as more than just a component of physical health; it stands as a pillar supporting comprehensive well-being and recovery.

Creating a Personalized Nutrition Plan

In the journey of recovery from Complex PTSD, individualized dietary approaches can play a pivotal role in enhancing emotional well-being. Crafting a nutrition plan that aligns with personal health needs and preferences is a fundamental step towards sustained recovery. One of the most effective ways to ensure this tailored approach is by consulting a nutritionist. Working alongside a qualified nutrition professional allows individuals to have their unique nutritional requirements and lifestyle habits meticulously evaluated. They provide expertise not only in crafting meal plans but also in educating on how various nutrients can influence mood and energy levels, which are crucial aspects when managing PTSD.

Nutritionists can help identify deficiencies that may exacerbate emotional distress and suggest foods rich in essential vitamins and minerals. This personalized guidance is invaluable because it takes into account individual differences in metabolism, allergies, or sensitivities, alongside mental health considerations. For instance, some individuals might benefit from an increased intake of omega-3 faȮy acids, known for their mood-stabilizing properties, while others may need to focus on improving gut health through probiotics. A nutritionist's insight ensures these specific needs are met, ultimately supporting both physical health and emotional stability.

Beyond professional consultation, self-discovery in food preferences is another vital aspect of developing a successful dietary plan for PTSD recovery. This involves a journey of exploring which foods bring joy and comfort without compromising health. Engaging in this process helps individuals connect with their bodies and emotions, fostering a deeper understanding of how certain foods affect their mood. It is an empowering experience that encourages mindful decision-making, allowing people to take control of their diet in a way that feels intrinsically rewarding. Experimentation with different types of cuisines and ingredients can uncover hidden favorites that resonate with one's emotional state, creating a sense of delight and satisfaction during meals.

This exploration aligns perfectly with the practice of mindful eating. By focusing on the sensory experiences of eating — the aroma, texture, taste, and even the sounds of food — individuals can cultivate a positive relationship with food. Mindful eating encourages slowing down and savoring each bite, which not only enhances enjoyment but also aids digestion and nutrient absorption. It shifts the focus from merely consuming nutrients to appreciating the act of eating itself as a nurturing, holistic experience. As individuals engage in mindful eating, they become more aÉuned to hunger signals and emotional triggers associated with food, enabling them to make beÉer food choices aligned with their healing journey.

Mindful eating practices can be supported by seÉing a calming environment for meals, free from distractions such as television or mobile devices. Some may find value in adopting rituals around mealtime, such as expressing gratitude for the food before them. These practices foster a sense of peace and mindfulness, reinforcing a healthy connection between food and emotional well-being. Gradually, individuals learn to identify how different foods make them feel physically and emotionally, paving the way for more conscious and joyful eating behaviors.

Tailored dietary approaches are essential because they significantly contribute to long-term adherence and emotional healing. Every person's path to recovery is unique, and so should be their nutritional strategies. Generic diets often fail to address the complexities of PTSD recovery, missing out on the nuances needed to support mental health. Personalized plans respect individual preferences and challenges, making it easier to integrate healthy eating habits into daily life sustainably. Consistency in following a nutrition plan is critical; thus, tailoring these plans ensures they are realistic and enjoyable, increasing the likelihood of them being maintained over time.

Moreover, personalized nutrition plans can adapt as recovery progresses. What works at one stage of healing may need adjustment as new goals are set or as the body's response changes. This adaptability is an asset in navigating the dynamic nature of PTSD recovery. Regular follow-ups with healthcare providers, including nutritionists, can facilitate these adjustments, helping individuals continue to derive maximum benefit from their dietary choices.

Finally, the impact of nutrition extends beyond the individual, reaching into their community of support. Family members and friends who understand and participate in the individualized nutritional journey can offer encouragement and accountability, creating a supportive network. This collective effort can enhance motivation and foster a shared commitment to health and well-being. Involving loved ones in meal planning or preparation can also be a bonding experience, enriching relationships and providing additional emotional nourishment.

Integrating Movement and Diet for Holistic Recovery

The journey to recovery from Complex PTSD is intricate, requiring a combination of strategies that cater to both mental and physical well-being. One effective approach involves integrating exercise with nutrition, which together provide a holistic path to healing. This synergy addresses the body and mind simultaneously, offering compounded benefits that can significantly enhance mental health.

The concept of synergistic effects highlights how exercise routines paired with healthy eating amplify mental health benefits. Exercise acts as a natural mood booster, releasing endorphins that help alleviate anxiety and depression symptoms commonly associated with PTSD. When complemented by a nutritious diet, these effects are magnified. Foods rich in essential nutrients like omega-3 faÉy acids and antioxidants support brain function, reducing inflammation and stabilizing mood swings. Regular physical activity coupled with balanced meals creates an environment where the body's stress response is beÉer managed, enhancing emotional regulation and mental resilience.

These practices not only offer immediate benefits but also encourage lifestyle changes that support sustainable well-being. By integrating exercise and nutrition into daily routines, individuals lay the groundwork for lasting habits that nurture both body and mind. This holistic approach transcends quick fixes, fostering a deeper commitment to self-care. Engaging in regular physical activities, like walking or yoga, alongside mindful eating cultivates consistency and routine, vital components for long-term recovery. Such integration transforms wellness goals into a lifestyle, promoting enduring health benefits beyond the realm of PTSD management.

Importantly, support systems play a crucial role in this integrated approach. Community resources and social networks can provide invaluable encouragement and accountability, making the journey less daunting. Participating in group fitness classes, cooking workshops, or community gardens can foster connections and shared experiences. These interactions build a sense of belonging and support, alleviating feelings of isolation that often accompany PTSD. Leveraging existing community structures offers an avenue for sustained motivation and companionship, reinforcing the commitment to holistic health practices.

Lastly, the long-term benefits of combining exercise with nutrition in managing PTSD symptoms cannot be overstated. This dual approach not only addresses physical and mental health challenges but also paves the way for transformative personal growth. Over time, individuals may notice improvements in energy levels, sleep quality, and overall mood stability, enhancing their capacity to cope with stressors. The enduring nature of these advantages underscores the value of this integrated strategy, offering hope and empowerment to those on their recovery journey.

Integrating anti-inflammatory foods into one's diet is another crucial component of this approach, warranting special attention. Consuming foods such as leafy greens, berries, and fatty fish helps reduce bodily inflammation, which has been linked to improved mental health outcomes. Offering practical guidelines, like incorporating a serving of green vegetables and oily fish into weekly meal plans, can make these dietary adjustments more accessible. Encouraging the exploration of diverse recipes and cooking methods ensures variety and enjoyment, making it easier to sustain these healthy eating habits over time.

Hydration is equally important, as maintaining optimal fluids plays a role in cognitive function and mental clarity. Adequate water intake supports focus and concentration, mitigating the cognitive disturbances often experienced by those with PTSD. Simple practices such as carrying a reusable water bottle and setting daily hydration goals can assist in developing consistent drinking habits. These small changes cumulatively contribute to a clearer, more alert mind, supporting overall recovery efforts.

Creating a personalized nutrition plan tailored to individual preferences and needs further reinforces the intersection of diet and mental health. Collaborating with nutritionists or dietitians can provide valuable insights, aligning dietary choices with personal goals and constraints. This personalized approach fosters a positive relationship with food, emphasizing mindful eating practices that honor both nutritional needs and taste preferences. Tailored plans ensure sustainability and adherence, maximizing the therapeutic potential of nutrition in PTSD recovery.

Support Systems and Resources

Building robust support systems and effectively utilizing available resources are essential steps in the recovery journey for individuals with Complex PTSD. This chapter delves into the profound impact that finding and engaging with supportive communities can have on one's path to healing. By exploring various avenues of support, individuals can alleviate feelings of isolation and gain strength from shared experiences. It's about finding those connections where understanding is mutual and victories are celebrated together, creating a network of care around those who might otherwise feel alone in their struggles.

Finding Support Groups

Complex PTSD, an intricate and challenging condition, often leaves individuals feeling isolated and misunderstood. One of the most powerful steps towards recovery is connecting with others who share similar experiences. Engaging with peer support groups can be immensely beneficial in this regard, providing emotional validation and a shared sense of belonging. Within these groups, participants can openly express their emotions, knowing they are among people who truly comprehend their struggles.

For many with Complex PTSD, the journey to healing can feel like navigating a labyrinth. Peer support groups act as guiding lanterns within this maze, illuminating paths through shared narratives and mutual understanding. When individuals hear stories that resonate with their own, it reinforces the validity of their experiences and nurtures an affirming environment where vulnerability is met with empathy rather than skepticism.

Sharing experiences with others facing similar challenges plays a crucial role in alleviating feelings of isolation. The silent burden borne by many with Complex PTSD can become lighter through collective sharing. These group settings offer a safe space for members to voice fears and victories alike, ensuring that they are not alone in their battles. In this camaraderie, individuals often find solace and comfort, realizing that their journey is intertwined with those of others who walk parallel paths.

Understanding that others face similar struggles can significantly enhance hope and motivation for recovery. Witnessing the resilience and progress of peers can inspire individuals to embrace their own healing journey with renewed vigor. As stories of perseverance and triumph are shared, they serve as living proof that healing is achievable. This exchange of hope and encouragement fosters a positive mindset, reinforcing the belief that overcoming adversity is possible with time and effort.

Furthermore, support groups can provide practical advice and coping strategies specifically tailored to the unique challenges of Complex PTSD. The richness of experiences within these groups offers diverse perspectives on managing symptoms and navigating daily life. Practical insights gained from those who have walked a similar path can prove invaluable for those seeking effective ways to cope. Whether it's mindfulness techniques or grounding exercises, these shared strategies form a toolkit that members can draw upon during difficult times.

The collective wisdom found in these circles often extends beyond theoretical discussion, transforming into actionable guidance. Members might learn about specific therapeutic practices that have helped others, which they can then incorporate into their own self-care routine. This exchange of knowledge not only enhances individual recovery efforts but also strengthens the collective resilience of the group.

As individuals with Complex PTSD participate in these supportive environments, it transforms their recovery journey from one of solitude to solidarity. Support groups encourage open dialogue, where fears are understood and hopes are amplified. By connecting with peers, individuals find not only validation but also inspiration, fostering an environment ripe for personal growth and healing.

The profound impact of engaging in peer support transcends mere conversation. It offers a tangible sense of community—a network of understanding hearts that uplifts each member. As rapport builds, these groups can evolve into deeply bonded communities where longstanding connections offer continual support. It's within this nurturing environment that individuals often discover new dimensions of themselves, stripped of judgment and surrounded by acceptance.

By actively participating in support groups, individuals practice the art of giving and receiving support. Sharing one's story becomes a tool for healing, both for the storyteller and the listener. This reciprocal process cultivates empathy and breaks down barriers of isolation, paving the way for stronger interpersonal connections.

Moreover, the benefits extend to family and friends of those with Complex PTSD. Observing the positive changes that arise from these groups can offer reassurance to loved ones, reaffirming that their support is part of a broader network aiding the individual's recovery. As individuals gain confidence and insight from their peers, they bring newfound understanding into their relationships, enhancing communication and closeness with those who care about them.

Mental health professionals, too, can benefit from understanding the dynamics within support groups. These gatherings showcase the power of peer-led initiatives in facilitating healing and resilience, reinforcing the importance of integrative approaches in therapy. By incorporating insights gained from peer interactions, therapists can beĖer tailor their strategies to meet the nuanced needs of individuals with Complex PTSD.

Types of Support Groups

In the journey of healing from Complex PTSD, support groups can play a pivotal role by offering individuals a safe space to explore their emotions and share experiences. Various formats of these groups are available, each with its unique characteristics and advantages.

In-person support groups are often highly valued for the powerful connections they foster through face-to-face interactions. Engaging directly with others who have similar experiences allows participants to bond over shared feelings and struggles. This personal connection can create an environment of trust where members feel more comfortable opening up about their thoughts and emotions. For example, many find solace in knowing they are not alone in their experiences, which can significantly aid in reducing feelings of isolation. Activities such as group discussions, expressive arts therapy, and collaborative exercises act as catalysts for forming deeper relationships among participants, enriching the healing process. Being physically present with others can also provide immediate emotional support, offering a sense of belonging that is vital for recovery.

On the other hand, online support groups bring their own set of benefits, primarily centered around convenience and accessibility. These virtual platforms break geographical barriers, allowing individuals from all over the world to connect at any time. The anonymity offered by online groups can be particularly beneficial for those who might feel apprehensive about sharing personal details in a face-to-face seEing. This feature empowers participants to disclose their stories openly, without fear of judgment, leading to honest exchanges that promote healing. Additionally, online groups offer flexibility in scheduling, making it easier for individuals to fit participation into their daily lives, regardless of work or familial obligations. Many online platforms also provide resources such as webinars, chat rooms, and curated content tailored to the needs of individuals with Complex PTSD, thus expanding their scope of support.

Specialized support groups cater to specific demographics, ensuring that the assistance provided is relevant and targeted. These groups might focus on survivors of childhood trauma, veterans, or individuals from particular cultural backgrounds, providing space for members to connect with others who truly understand their unique challenges. By tailoring the discussion topics and activities to reflect the shared experiences of the group, participants can engage more deeply with the material. For instance, a group dedicated to childhood trauma survivors may address issues like rebuilding trust and managing parental relationships, offering tools and insights specific to these concerns. Having a specialized focus enhances the group's effectiveness, as members are more likely to relate to one another's stories and learn coping strategies that are directly applicable to their situations.

Professional-led support groups blend the benefits of peer interaction with expert guidance. Under the supervision of trained facilitators—such as psychologists or counselors—these groups ensure that discussions proceed within a structured framework. Facilitators can introduce therapeutic techniques and guide conversations in ways that maximize therapeutic outcomes. They often provide insights based on professional knowledge, helping participants to reframe negative thought patterns and develop healthier coping mechanisms. Moreover, having a professional present ensures that any emerging psychological distress can be swiftly addressed, maintaining a safe environment for all involved. These groups typically follow evidence-based approaches, fostering a structured yet supportive atmosphere conducive to personal growth.

For many individuals with Complex PTSD, the choice between these support group formats hinges on personal preference and specific needs. Some may thrive in the physical presence of others, finding comfort in tangible interaction, while others might prefer the flexibility and anonymity of an online setup. Specialized groups offer niche environments that cater to distinct experiences, whereas professional-led groups provide a balanced mix of peer support and expert input. Ultimately, what matters most is that individuals have access to a format that resonates with them, enabling them to harness the full potential of their support network.

How to Find a Support Group

In the complex landscape of recovery from Complex PTSD, finding suitable support systems can be a transformative step. National organizations serve as a cornerstone for those navigating this journey. These organizations often maintain directories that are invaluable resources, listing local and online support groups dedicated to Complex PTSD. Resources like the National Alliance on Mental Illness (NAMI) or the Anxiety and Depression Association of America often host these directories, offering a starting point for anyone seeking supportive communities. These directories categorize groups by region and focus, making it easier to find those fiEing specific needs or experiences.

Utilizing such directories can be particularly beneficial due to the comprehensive nature in which they are maintained. They typically include information about the meeting styles, such as whether they are virtual, in-person, or hybrid, which can accommodate various preferences and comfort levels. For individuals who are isolated geographically or have mobility issues, online groups listed in these directories provide an accessible option. Moreover, national organizations often vet these listings, ensuring that they uphold certain standards of care and professionalism. This reassurance is vital, particularly for individuals new to seeking help for Complex PTSD.

Another key resource in identifying appropriate support groups lies in leveraging the expertise of mental health professionals. Whether it's a therapist, counselor, or psychiatrist, these professionals are often equipped with knowledge of reputable support groups that align with their clients' specific therapeutic goals and emotional requirements. Having direct conversations with mental health providers about joining a group can open doors to specialized networks, such as those focused on trauma survivors or specific symptoms related to Complex PTSD.

Mental health clinicians can provide insights into the structure and dynamics of different groups. For example, some may emphasize cognitive-behavioral techniques, while others might offer a more exploratory approach focusing on personal narratives and shared experiences. Engaging with these insights allows individuals to choose a group that not only meets their logistical needs but also complements their therapeutic objectives and personal healing style. This tailored approach ensures that participants feel understood and supported in environments conducive to their unique challenges and growth paths.

The digital world offers vast opportunities for connection through online forums and mental health apps. Platforms like The Mighty, Reddit, or specialized apps developed specifically for mental health support can connect individuals with forums that resonate deeply with their lived experiences. These spaces often foster a sense of community among users, where people freely share stories, advice, and encouragement. Apps specifically designed for mental health can guide users in locating active, engaging communities that are empathetic and knowledgeable about Complex PTSD. Such platforms often include features that allow members to filter discussions or search for specific topics, making it easier to dive into areas of interest or concern.

These online communities provide flexibility and accessibility, accommodating those who might be unable to aÉend regular meetings due to scheduling conflicts or geographical limitations. Participating in online forums also grants a level of anonymity, which can be critical for individuals who may feel apprehensive about disclosing personal details face-to-face. Here, members can engage at their own pace, contributing during moments of crisis or when they feel ready to share their stories.

Word-of-mouth referrals remain a powerful tool in uncovering hidden gems within the support group ecosystem. Trusted friends, family members, or fellow survivors often have firsthand experience with local support groups, offering insights that directories or online searches may not capture. Personal recommendations frequently carry additional weight because they come from individuals who understand the nuances of

Complex PTSD and can vouch for the supportive environment of a particular group.

Such referrals not only guide individuals to reputed groups but also foster a sense of community before even stepping into a session. Knowing someone personally who has engaged with a group adds a layer of familiarity and assurance that can alleviate hesitations about joining a new collective. Moreover, hearing testimonials about the tangible benefits others have experienced, such as reduced symptoms or increased resilience, reinforces the potential impact these support networks can have.

Community Resources for Ongoing Assistance

Navigating the path to recovery from Complex PTSD involves more than just personal resolve; it requires a robust support system comprised of accessible local resources and community services. These resources can collectively form a safety net, providing continuous support and fostering resilience.

For many individuals, counseling services are a cornerstone of the recovery process. Across various communities, free or sliding-scale counseling options are available, specifically tailored for trauma survivors. These services ensure that financial constraints do not become barriers to receiving essential mental health support. Local health departments or nonprofit organizations often run these programs, making them accessible to many. Sessions with trained professionals provide a safe space to unpack traumatic experiences, learn coping mechanisms, and work towards healing in a supportive environment. Counselors specializing in trauma can help individuals navigate the complexities of their experiences, offering personalized strategies and techniques that address unique challenges.

During particularly challenging moments, crisis hotlines serve as a lifeline, offering immediate emotional support and guidance. Available 24/7, these hotlines are staffed by compassionate, trained individuals who can listen, provide reassurance, and suggest practical next steps. The anonymity and immediacy of hotline services remove the pressure some might feel when seeking help in person. Moreover, these services are vital during moments of acute distress, providing instant access to a non-judgmental ear and helpful advice that can make a significant difference in how a crisis is navigated.

Many community centers offer wellness classes such as yoga or art therapy, which play a crucial role in promoting overall well-being for those with Complex PTSD. These activities address both physical and psychological needs, with yoga focusing on breath control, relaxation, and gentle movement to foster mindfulness and calmness. On the other hand, art therapy provides an expressive outlet for emotions that may be difficult to articulate verbally. By participating in creative endeavors, individuals can explore complex feelings and insights in a supportive group setting. These classes not only help in reducing symptoms of anxiety and depression associated with PTSD but also empower individuals by fostering new skills and hobbies that contribute positively to their recovery journey.

Libraries and local universities can be treasure troves of knowledge and learning opportunities. Many offer free courses and lectures focused on mental health topics, equipping attendees with valuable insights into understanding and managing Complex PTSD. Libraries often host workshops and discussions led by experts, creating an inclusive environment where participants can ask questions and gain clarity on subjects relevant to their experiences. Universities, too, frequently open up public lecture series featuring leading researchers and practitioners in psychology and mental health. Attending these educational events serves dual purposes: enhancing understanding of the condition while simultaneously building a sense of community among aÉendees who share similar interests and concerns.

A key aspect of effectively utilizing these resources lies in knowing how to access them. Start by reaching out to local health providers or community centers for information about available services. Websites of local governments or nonprofit organizations can also list current programs and contact details. Additionally, networking within community groups or online forums can lead to word-of-mouth recommendations for under-the-radar resources that have worked well for others in similar situations.

When considering joining any resource or service, it's important to reflect on your own needs and comfort levels. For instance, if social interaction is currently overwhelming, beginning with anonymous resources like hotlines might feel safer before aÉempting in-person classes or workshops. It's also beneficial to review testimonials or feedback from past participants to gauge the effectiveness of a particular service.

Moreover, keep in mind the importance of consistent involvement to maximize benefits. Recovery is not always linear, and engaging with multiple resources over time can build a comprehensive framework for healing. Regular participation in therapies, continuous learning through courses, and maintaining connections established at community centers can significantly contribute to a more resilient recovery process.

Therapeutic Services and Self-Help Resources

When embarking on a journey toward healing from Complex PTSD, the importance of finding an appropriate therapist cannot be overstressed. A therapist with expertise in trauma-informed care understands the nuances of how traumatic experiences affect the mind and body. This specialized knowledge enables them to tailor their approach to meet the unique needs of individuals facing Complex PTSD. Whether through Cognitive Behavioral Therapy, EMDR, or somatic therapies, these professionals bring a wealth of tools designed to support recovery by directly addressing trauma-specific challenges. When choosing a therapist, it is essential for individuals to consider compatibility, therapeutic style, and whether they feel supported and understood throughout their sessions.

Beyond individual therapy, group therapy settings present another valuable opportunity for healing. In these spaces, individuals come together under the guidance of a professional, fostering environments where shared experiences promote mutual growth. The collective nature of group therapy means that participants can provide and receive support from peers who understand their struggles. This setting encourages open dialogue and creates a sense of community—a crucial factor in overcoming feelings of isolation commonly associated with Complex PTSD. Group therapy also allows members to witness diverse coping strategies and cultivate empathy as they hear others sharing their journeys.

For those seeking self-guided resources, self-help literature stands as a pillar of personal development. Books focusing on trauma recovery not only educate readers about their condition but also offer practical strategies for managing symptoms. These texts are wriÉen by experts who share insights into the processes of healing and resilience-building. By delving into these works, individuals gain a deeper understanding of the complexities of their experiences and are inspired to pursue personal growth proactively. Furthermore, stories of recovery within these pages serve as a beacon of hope, illustrating that healing, while challenging, is indeed aÉainable.

In addition to books, engaging with educational podcasts or webinars can significantly bolster ongoing resilience and knowledge. These formats allow individuals to connect with new research and recovery strategies, keeping them informed and empowered. Podcasts bring voices of experts right to one's ears, offering conversational insights into advancements in trauma care. Webinars often provide interactive elements, allowing aÉendees to ask questions and engage more deeply with the material presented. Such accessibility means that learning and growth can continue regardless of location, further expanding opportunities for personal empowerment.

To maximize the benefits of these resources, it is useful for individuals to explore a combination of both professional support and self-help materials. This blended approach ensures continuous growth by integrating structured guidance with personal exploration. By building a diverse support network that includes therapists, peers in group seÉings, and the vast array of self-help resources available, individuals can create a comprehensive system tailored to their unique needs. Embracing a variety of resources strengthens resilience, equipping individuals with the tools necessary to navigate the complexities of their recovery journey.

CONCLUSION

As you reach the final pages of this guide, take a moment to breathe deeply and reflect on the path you've traversed. This book has been a companion in your exploration of Complex PTSD, providing insights, strategies, and encouragement along your journey. Whether you're someone personally navigating the complexities of this condition, a caring friend or family member, or a dedicated mental health professional, acknowledging your progress is essential. Each page turned represents a step forward—a small victory that contributes to significant change.

Throughout our chapters together, we've delved into the distinctive nuances that separate PTSD from Complex PTSD, shedding light on the causes and symptoms that may be impacting your life or the lives of those you care for. Understanding these differences is crucial. It empowers you with the knowledge to address specific challenges with more precision and empathy. We've also explored various emotional regulation techniques, offering tools that can help ease intense emotions when they threaten to overwhelm. These techniques form the bedrock of resilience, allowing you to rebuild a sense of stability and control amidst chaos.

Central to our discussions was the transformative power of rewriting our narratives. Life's stories, particularly those intertwined with trauma, often come steeped in pain and struggle. Yet, through conscious effort, we can reframe these narratives, allowing healing to begin. By embracing new perspectives, you can find meaning where there once was only despair, thereby fostering hope and renewal. Remember, reframing isn't about forgeÉing the past; it's about changing how it influences your present and future.

As we part ways, carry with you the understanding that recovery from Complex PTSD is not a linear journey nor is it a destination with a definitive end. It's an ever-evolving process characterized by gradual healing and ongoing growth. The tools and insights gained here are just the beginning.

As you continue on this path, seek out additional resources to nurture your development further. Books, workshops, therapy sessions, and community engagements can continually enrich your perspective and add depth to your healing repertoire.

In moving forward, consider how establishing a robust support network can significantly impact your recovery journey. No one should face the struggles of Complex PTSD alone. Emotional connections provide anchor points, making the turbulent waters of healing more navigable. Reach out to friends and family members who understand your experiences and can offer comfort and validation. Their presence can be a soothing balm during times of distress and a source of motivation when your own energy wanes.

Support groups offer another avenue of connectivity. In these circles, shared stories create a tapestry of commonality, knitting together individuals who have faced similar trials. Within the safe space of such groups, vulnerability transforms into strength, enabling participants to share lessons learned and celebrate victories, both large and small. If participating in person feels daunting, explore online communities where anonymity can sometimes make sharing easier.

Mental health professionals remain invaluable allies in this journey. Their expertise provides a guiding light, helping to navigate complex and sometimes treacherous paths. Therapists can introduce therapeutic techniques specifically tailored to Complex PTSD, while continually adjusting approaches based on feedback and progress. Remember that finding the right therapist is a personal journey itself—one requiring patience and perseverance. A good therapeutic relationship can feel like a lifeline during challenging stretches.

Finally, as you move beyond this book, hold onto the core belief that transformative change is possible. The initial steps may feel daunting, but each stride builds upon the last, creating momentum toward healing. Celebrate every breakthrough, no matter how seemingly insignificant, they contribute to a cumulative transformation that shapes a resilient future.

Encourage yourself to embrace self-compassion when setbacks occur, viewing them as opportunities for learning rather than failures.

The landscape of healing from Complex PTSD is vast and varied, and while this guide provides a roadmap, your journey will be uniquely yours. Tailor what you've learned to fit your individual needs, and don't hesitate to innovate. Healing is not a measurement of time but of progress and understanding. Draw strength from your accomplishments, glean insights from your experiences, and envision a future where peace and fulfillment reside at the forefront of your narrative.

Embrace this standpoint with an open heart, aware that everyone's journey unfolds differently. Whether you're piecing together fragmented memories, standing beside a loved one as they rebuild, or offering guidance as a professional, remember the profound impact of empathy, patience, and persistence. By commiEing fully to this path, you not only heal yourself but also pave the way for others to follow in your footsteps.

So, as you close this chapter, remind yourself of the courage it took to confront these topics. Your willingness to engage reflects immense strength and character. Let this book serve as both a testament to your resilience and a beacon lighting the path ahead. With knowledge and support, you're equipped to face whatever comes next. May your journey be filled with understanding, growth, and the kind of enduring healing that transforms not just moments but lifetimes.

Scan the QR code to claim your free bonus resource now!

2025 PTSD & TRAUMA WORKBOOK

www.ingramcontent.com/pod-product-compliance
Lightning Source LLC
Chambersburg PA
CBHW061051250726
48653CB00001B/352